GENEVA
ON THE LAKE

A HISTORY OF OHIO'S
FIRST SUMMER RESORT

WENDY KOILE

Charleston — London

THE
History
PRESS

Published by The History Press
Charleston, SC 29403
www.historypress.net

First published 2012

Manufactured in the United States

ISBN 978.1.60949.487.2

Library of Congress Cataloging-in-Publication Data

Koile, Wendy.
Geneva on the Lake : a history of Ohio's first summer resort / Wendy Koile.
p. cm.
Includes bibliographical references.
ISBN 978-1-60949-487-2
1. Geneva-on-the-Lake (Ohio)--History. 2. Summer resorts--Ohio--Geneava-on-
the-Lake--History. I. Title.
F499.G443K65 2012
977.1'34--dc23
2012001589

To my Grandpa and Grandma Eberly.
Thanks for all the memories.

CONTENTS

PREFACE

C rammed into the backseat with my sister, a heap of bedding between us, I am barely tolerating the drive. Just as most children await the arrival of Christmas Day, I have yearned for this Sunday in August all year. After what seems like hours, we finally crest the little hill on State Route 534. Just at that moment, my stomach begins to turn summersaults. For it is then that I get my first glimpse of Lake Erie. I will have a full week ahead of me with my family in my favorite place in the whole world.

Fast-forward twenty-five years: I am cruising along this same stretch of road, with my little girl singing in the backseat. I keep my eyes directly ahead, as I do not want to miss that moment. After all this time, my stomach still flips over the minute I see that turquoise blue border.

I have often wondered what it is that makes my time at Geneva on the Lake (GOTL) so meaningful. Is it the combination of the bright lights, delicious food and spectacular attractions? Perhaps it's the time spent relaxing on the beach. Maybe it's simply the pleasure of being on vacation.

Yes, those things certainly intrigue me. Yet there is something more. At GOTL, my best childhood memories are relived every year. The best laughs of my life. The best of times spent with my entire extended family, crowded into one cabin. The best home-cooked meals courtesy of my grandparents. The best times I have ever had! It is only at GOTL that I am able to capture those same feelings again and again.

Throughout this research process, I have met so many people with similar heartfelt stories. From all the GOTL fans I have met, I have learned that every person holds on to his or her own special memories. Most, like me, continue to bring their children to GOTL in the hopes of re-creating those magical memories. I believe that all of us will always experience butterflies in our stomachs as we arrive at our favorite place.

It was with great pleasure that I embarked on the exciting task of preserving the history of this resort town that has come to live in my heart. It was never my intention to become the town expert or town historian. Instead, I wished to become a storyteller for a town that has an amazing story to tell. Indeed, my best inspiration for writing comes from my own family's vacations at the lake, covering four generations and counting. Therefore, I am simply a Geneva on the Lake vacationer, exploring, organizing and sharing this story about Ohio's first resort.

ACKNOWLEDGEMENTS

I would like to thank my commissioning editor, Joe Gartrell. You heard my idea and believed in it from day one. I would also like to thank everyone at The History Press whose expertise made my project into a book.

This project could not have been successful without the help of many who, in my opinion, do bear the titles of experts and/or historians. A special thanks is given to the late Jean Metcalf of the Ashtabula Historical Society, who offered me all the help she could provide. Whether it be answering my questions or giving me full access to the museum, Jean was more than helpful in the research process.

Another special thanks goes to John D. "Jack" Sargent, who enthusiastically and kindly shared his knowledge and GOTL collection of artifacts (and to his wife, Sara Jane, for allowing him to store all "his stuff" in their beautiful home). Jack's sense of humor and fun approach to sharing his recollections of "back in the day" was definitely one of the highlights of this research project.

A warm thank-you to Jim Lavender, who helped me anytime I asked. I not only found a good reference but a dear friend as well.

Yet another thanks goes to my new friend, Glenn Beagle, at the Ashtabula Maritime Museum, who spent hours sharing his love and knowledge of the Lake.

I would like to thank Barbara Hamilton, who kindly shared her own research with me.

Thanks to Mark Brunner and his parents, who shared with me their memories and love for GOTL. There is "no place in the world like it."

And to the many other friends I've met throughout this process, including the Bushes at the Eagle Cliff, Marge Milliken at the Geneva on the Lake Chamber of Commerce, the Geneva Library historians, the Ashtabula County Library Reference Department, Lynn at CSU library, DAFE, the Norton auctioneers, Kathy Collins, Joe Parry, Jack Schmitt, Mike Hanson, Martha Woodward, local business owners and any other locals I may have "bugged" along the way, thank you! So many people offered support and encouragement. I could not have continued without you.

Thanks to my friends and co-workers who never questioned my ability to write a book. Your support meant so much to me.

Most of all, I would like to thank my wonderful family, who believed in me all along.

CHAPTER 1

SETTLING IN

S ilently, a small cluster of people stood gazing out across an expansive blue lake. For weeks now, they had explored these new lands, encountering trees as wide as their cabins back home, wild creatures like never known before, a lake that could be calm one moment and a raging sea the next and extreme geographical features that sometimes presented unforgiving obstacles. But these people had a job to do here. They were there to survey and map out these strange new lands. And no mosquito-infested swamp or monstrous trees would stand in their way. Because sometime in the midst of toiling through treacherous landscapes and completing backbreaking duties, these people came to realize that it was worth the hardship. The team recognized that on these lands nature had provided a wealth of riches like never before experienced. From an abundance of game to breathtaking sunsets, these strange yet undeniably beautiful lands would come to be known as "home" to thousands of future settlers.

THE WESTERN RESERVE

Shortly after the Revolutionary War, the State of Connecticut, in exchange for the construction of public schools in its own state, had agreed to give up its landholdings in northeast Ohio, then known as the Connecticut Western Reserve. In 1795, the state sold this land to the Connecticut Land

Trees and vegetation still grow along the lakeshore at GOTL today. The lake is barely visible through the growth, as it would have been in the days of the settlers. *Author's collection.*

Company for $1.2 million, or about $0.40 per acre. The following year, Moses Cleaveland and a band of surveyors were sent from Connecticut to begin surveying and drawing up townships in the Reserve.

THE JOURNEY

The team was made up of a leader, Cleaveland, six surveyors and several chain axe-men and their wives and children—about fifty in total. They also had about a dozen horse and cattle. Some of the party chose to travel to the Reserve mostly by way of supply boat. Others went overland and kept careful account of the journey. At one point, near the present-day Ohio border, the two parties were separated for several days. The boats did not appear at the designated meeting place, causing great concern for those waiting on land.

Apparently, after sailing the Niagara River and then into Lake Erie, the crew met with a devastating storm that destroyed and damaged several boats in the caravan. John Milton Holley recorded that "on Saturday morning there sprang up in the northwest a storm, and blew most violently on the shores of the Lake. This proved fatal to one of the boats, and damaged another very much, though we went forward to a safe harbor, and built several fires on the bank of the Lake as a beacon to those coming on."

Eventually, both parties were reunited on the mouth of Conneaut Creek, which flows into Lake Erie. This would be the first stop in the Western Reserve. On July 4, 1795, exactly twenty years after America earned its declaration of freedom, the crew celebrated its arrival. Here they prayed for and blessed the land as they dipped into the fresh, cool water from the lake.

On these shores, nature ran wild, including thousands of huge elm and oak trees. Animals, some that were thought extinct at the time, enjoyed the peaceful area where they had easy access to fresh water. Some Native Americans were thought to be still lingering in the area. Before the Revolution, they had been pushed to the land west of the Cuyahoga River. However, some small tribes remained in the area, peacefully moving and hunting about the lands.

After resting and recuperating from the hellish storm, surely one of Lake Erie's infamous whoppers, the crew continued on down the lakeshore, surveying and recording townships. As the team made its way farther into the Reserve, the members were met with unfavorable conditions. Swamps, unstable ground, rocks and ridges relentlessly appeared in the heavily wooded areas. At one point, the surveyors crossed through a swamp chest deep. This passage through the huge swamp would take a day's worth of travel. John Milton Holley recorded in his journal, "In the night, I began to grow sick at my stomach, and soon vomited up everything that was in me. Mr. Pease too had a turn of the cramp, in consequence of traveling all day in the water."

Hardships, sickness, mosquito swarms and unstable weather continued to be part of daily life. However, in spite of these conditions, this team carried on in its quest. What did this land that contained "the most abominable swamp" have to offer these people? Maybe it came down to work ethic. These folks were from a generation that had taken part in building the colonies. To toil day and night was not necessarily a new concept. Perhaps this crew was ready to follow through on a creed. After all, many of these men, including their leader, had just soldiered in the Revolutionary War. These very lands were what the veterans had agreed to give their lives for not so long ago.

Or maybe, on one of those evenings after sledging through the mud and muck, they sat on the lakeshore gazing across the purple-blue water. Something about it just felt right. This land with its acres of timber, abundant fish and wildlife and sparkling water had a serenity about it that was like no other. Yes, this land would be a place that their fellow countrymen could visit to find not only bountifulness in provisions but also the quiet peacefulness that seemed to surround the lakeshore.

So, with great perseverance, the team pushed forward all the way to the Cuyahoga River. They named the land near the river's edge Cleaveland after their ever-encouraging leader. (Later the "a" would be dropped in an attempt to save room in news printing endeavors.)

As the team ran low on certain supplies, and with a cold nip in the air beginning to filter in, they realized that they would have to return home. At this time, the township of Cleaveland, as well as several sections in the northeast corner of the Reserve, had been surveyed, mapped and marked. On October 1796, departing from Conneaut Creek, all but ten people sailed to Presque Isle and then home. The families who stayed, including small children, were left with the rest of the usable supplies. Although they faced a harsh Ohio winter, these families opted to stake a claim in the new land and begin cultivating some of the goodness that seemed to be watching and waiting within the deep forests.

Over the next several years, land in the Western Reserve would continue to be mapped and settled. In 1803, Ohio earned its official statehood. Droves of families filtered through the New England colonies and made their way to this new and exciting territory. Large blocks of land, known as townships, filled in quickly and peacefully. Interestingly, it would be the areas closest to the Lake Erie shoreline that would be settled last.

THE MYSTERIOUS SETTLERS

It is believed that before the first recorded settlement in GOTL, there may have been a small group that had attempted settling in the area. The group was made up of five or six families who roughly fashioned together log cabins. Within a short amount of time, for unknown reasons, the families abandoned this site and left their cabins to the harsh lakeshore elements. The group never returned to the area again.

Some historians have suggested that the group lived in the area sometime between 1810 and 1816. If true, they would have experienced some trying times for anyone living near the lakeshore. First, there was a little feud known as the War of 1812. One of the contributing factors of the war was the issue of British soldiers still living and perhaps dominating land along the Great Lakes. Also, both warring sides had desires for land in Canada, and this was a major factor in the tensions. Attempts were made to enter the Canadian borders from every angle. Thus, huge battles were fought on the waters of Lake Erie. Perry's warships would have passed right by the GOTL area.

A story, recorded in Ashtabula County's early history, recounts a tale of John Austin, a wheat farmer. As John was harvesting his crop near the lakeshore, he heard the distinct rumble of thunder across the lake. Knowing the potential ferociousness of a Lake Erie storm, John quickly finished his task at hand. However, the thundering never produced the storm. In fact, John watched the sun set on a very peaceful lake. A few days later, a courier rode through town announcing Perry's victory on the lake. John actually heard the thunderous sound of warships out across the lake.

The families living along the shores were affected by the feuding in other ways as well. Both armies, British and American, needed soldiers and sailors. Both sides needed food and shelter from the lake elements. And both sides held fast to the notion that these lands rightfully belonged to them. Perhaps the families living in the Geneva settlement opted to either hop aboard a ship and serve in an army or leave the land and head south for some peace and quiet.

Another speculation is that the first pioneers here would have experienced the "1816 Poverty Year" or the "Year Without a Summer." This strange weather anomaly was caused by heavy volcanic eruptions and strange climatic phenomena that occurred in the stratosphere. The outcome of this storm was a literal year without a summer, marked with frigid temperatures, snowstorms and ice-covered lakes. The July sun could not penetrate an eerily thick fog that slept night and day on all of northeast North America. Crops did not grow. Cabins roughly thrown together did not block the coldness from entering. Many people did not survive. Many people did not hang around to see if this was a normal occurrence.

Regardless of reasoning, these families did not stay for long, and it would be the next few pioneer families who would begin to create what is known as Geneva on the Lake, Ohio's first resort.

Welcome, Pioneers

As the Connecticut Land Company continued its ventures in the Reserve, the financial investors in the home state began business transactions concerning the newly mapped property. One such investor was Joseph Battell, along with his wife, Sarah. The Battells were known in their hometown as being kind and trustworthy members of the small town. So when Harvey S. Spencer learned that the Battells had land in the Reserve for sale, he jumped at the chance. The deed of his investment was dated February 20, 1818, for eighty acres of land overloaded with oak.

As Spencer and his family made the three-week journey across the states, another young entrepreneur and his family were busy at work in present-day GOTL. Solomon Fitch, who is believed to be the first residential landholder, had migrated to the land two years earlier in 1816, which is also the time the town was incorporated and set off from Harpersfiled. On his 1,300 acres of lakeshore property, near the present-day Jenny Munger Gregory Museum, Fitch built a log home for his family. Backed by the Connecticut Land Company, Fitch also constructed a pier and docking area from which he shipped lumber to nearby Ashtabula Harbor. The lumber was reloaded at the harbor and transported to Buffalo, New York

In 1823, Solomon Fitch's son, Thomas, built the first frame house, which he called Grandview; it would eventually become the Ashtabula Historical Society headquarters. Lumber from his father's business was used in the construction.

Meanwhile, Harvey Spencer and his family were settling in on the property adjacent to the Fitches. (Spencer's property is the modern-day Mapletown Beach area.) The gentlemen struck up a quick friendship that led to a business partnership. While Fitch worked clearing the white wood and white oak, Spencer worked at cutting the wood into barrel staves. Although the men ran a successful business, the work was difficult. The heavily wooded area was covered in oaks, walnut and chestnut trees, many five to six feet in diameter. However, the nearby shoreline was flat and sandy and provided easy access to the lake. Thus, the natural land features helped to create a well-working business.

Along with launching his cargo into the lake, Spencer realized that it was quite simple to release his personal water vessels. He soon began fishing expeditions in his flat-bottomed boat. On one of those journeys, Spencer hooked three humongous fish known as sturgeon. Spencer quickly realized that at certain times of the year, the sturgeon came to the shallow water for mating purposes. Being a sharp businessman, he quickly capitalized on this and sold the stock to travelers and neighbors. Many times, the monstrous fish would be hauled off in the back of a flat-bottomed wagon. For decades, the Spencer property would be known as Sturgeon Point.

It is interesting to note that at this time the early homesteads were set back at least one-fourth of a mile from the shore. The early settlers could not even see the lake, as the tree coverage and vegetation was incredibly thick. Plus, the trees provided shelter from the raging storms that arose quite frequently over the lake.

Over the next few decades, families continued to purchase, settle and clear the land in the area that is presently GOTL. Eventually, families discovered rich, fertile land as trees were cleared, leaving plenty of room for farming. Thus, families cultivated the lands and experienced great success with crops. One such family, who had also purchased land from the Battells, was the Reuben Warner family. Much history is recorded about this particular family due to the findings of present-day writer and historian Barbara Hamilton.

YARD SALE TREASURES

Mrs. Hamilton enjoys researching and writing articles about Ashtabula County history. Over a lifetime, she has collected many artifacts from the days of old. Frequently, she visits antique shops, flea markets and yard sales. It is somewhat of a treasure hunt as she browses through dusty piles of books, papers and trinkets in the hopes of finding a treasure from the past.

On a warm spring afternoon in 2005, Barbara found herself at a retired auctioneer's yard sale. As she made her way around card tables and crumbling boxes filled with items, she noticed on a table two small red leather-bound books. Other customers had passed by the worn-out books, but Barbara was instantly drawn to them. As she examined the books, she realized that they were diaries. She purchased the books for one dollar each and learned that they had come from an estate sale several years prior at the present-day Colonial Inn in GOTL.

Barbara hopped in her car and gingerly placed the little books on the front seat. As she drove home, she wondered about the diaries. She had learned from her initial skimming that they had belonged to Nelson and Laura Warner, dating 1895–97. But did they have any connection to Ashtabula County?

Barbara soon began her research and learned that the Warners were one of the first families to settle in the town of GOTL. The diaries were full of day-to-day life events. This family, who made their way to the area in 1828, would go on to greatly affect the little town. Barbara held in her hands a definite link to her county's history.

THE WARNERS MOVE TO TOWN

In 1828, Reuben and Maria Warner set off on a grueling journey to the Western Reserve. They, too, had purchased a tract of land from the Battells back in Connecticut. As newlyweds, they dreamed about the fertile new land

and the life that they would have there together. They happily loaded their wedding gifts, including a set of mulberry china, into an ox cart and headed out into the unknown.

After days of being en route, they came to a tiny village with a cluster of log houses. They soon located their parcel of land, which was so vast that it included the present-day golf course and most of today's business district. As they secured the wagon and looked about the area, they noticed the large log cabin to their northwest. Their new neighbors, the Fitches, would soon become dear friends.

As the couple settled in, they began harvesting the land and establishing a successful, working farm. The couple eventually had three children: Truman, Abigail and Nelson. Nelson married Laura Sullivan and had four children. The diaries found more than one hundred years later belonged to Nelson and Laura. The couple continued to manage the farm and later opened one of the first boardinghouses in the area.

Day-to-day life was filled with the work of maintaining a farm. Nelson kept careful mention of the hours upon hours dedicated to farming. Laura attended to the needs of the summer boarders and kept detailed records of the business. Through the diaries, readers can learn of the family's hard work and dedication to sustaining a business as well as a healthy family life. Following are some examples from the diaries.

The Warner Homestead in early boarding years. *Author's collection.*

Friday, January 1, 1897
31st anniversary of our wedding. Pleasant. Father and Mother Sullivan,
Byron and Ruby, Adasa and Bertha Hoskin were here to dinner. Chored 5
hours. Charlie worked on icehouse 3 hours. Charlie had corner post fall on
his hip which laid him up.

Tuesday, April 27, 1897
Time to look for chicks. The old hen concluded she would not set—so we
are minus the chicks. Pleasant but a little cool. Done chores 5½ hours.
Sowed grass seed on the oats ground. 6 hours. Charlie plowed 1½ acres. 7
hours. Got 27 eggs.

August 1, 1897
Milton's Family went home, Bassett and wife came to stay over another day.

SHIPPING AND MANUFACTURING

As permanent residency along the lakeshore increased, so did the concept of making a living by way of Lake Erie. Some, like Solomon Fitch and Harvey Spencer, had already discovered the benefit of utilizing the lake as a means of a livelihood. After all, the GOTL settlement was located right between several busy shipping ports, including Cleveland, Fairport, Ashtabula and Conneaut. Therefore, transporting goods would not be difficult.

A few years after Solomon Fitch built his docks and small sailing vessels, he learned that ships from Kelly's Island carrying limestone were docking at Cowles Creek, which was adjacent to his property. Something big was happening over at the creek, and Fitch soon came to play an important part in the business.

Apparently, on Great Lot #3 a family by the name of Granger had established a small lime burning business. The son, Francis Granger, was in charge of the business and was looking for a few good men to work for the family. Granger was aware of the successful business endeavors of the neighboring Fitch family. Not only was Fitch an intelligent businessman, he also evidently was skilled with handling money, as he was the township treasurer in 1823. At some point, Granger made Solomon Fitch head supervisor of the company. And so began one of GOTL's main industries of the time.

DISCOVERY AT COWLES CREEK

Fast-forward 160 years from the time of the lime burning business. A local amateur archaeologist had just recently researched the Cowles Creek role in early industry. As Ron Burr, a part-time resident, was exploring the

Above: Underground kiln structure during archaeological dig. *Kent State Library, Special Collections, Michael Kingsley Papers.*

Below: From above, the below-ground lime burning kiln. *Kent State Library, Special Collections, Michael Kingsley Papers.*

former Chestnut Grove area, he noticed a strange indentation on the wall of an eroding cliff. If this was what he thought it was, it was worth a more in-depth study.

Burr contacted Professor Ronald Kingsley at Kent State University. After gaining permits, the Kent State researchers began the process of rescuing the structure. Locals of the area were allowed to watch and ask questions as the study was performed. What Mr. Burr had found hiding in the hillside was determined to be one of the large lime burning kilns of the early 1800s.

Thanks to infamous wind and wave erosion ripping away the hillside, the buried kiln was exposed just enough for a curious explorer to discover. This type of kiln was built into the side of the hill and was most likely one of three for this business. Kingsley and his team measured it to be seven feet wide and six feet tall.

Lime was shipped from the lime mines on Kelly's Island. At Cowles Creek, the lime was burned and stored in barrels to be shipped. The lime was used to aid in construction using plaster or mortar. Many of the early buildings in GOTL are thought to have been built with the lime from Cowles Creek.

CANAL PROPOSAL

In 1908, in the early years of the Industrial Revolution, access to the Great Lakes was at the forefront of the minds of many businessmen. As shipping along the lake grew, so did the desire to utilize these waterways farther inland. Thus, officials sought to open a shipping canal, nearly one hundred miles long, stretching from the GOTL area to Pittsburgh.

Farmland was bought up by industrial tycoons in the future town of Geneva Harbor, near Cowles Creek. Jones and Laughlin Steel Company owners were eager to build at the head of the harbor, promising to be the largest steel factory in the world. In fact, promoters of Geneva Harbor declared that not only would this harbor town be as successful as Gary, Indiana, it would surely surpass it.

The Lake Erie and Pittsburg canal bed would need to be two hundred feet wide and eighteen feet deep in order to float the huge barges of the lake, some of which carried two thousand tons. This new route would not only link Pittsburg to Lake Erie, but it would also link Pittsburg to the Ohio River.

As the years wore on, and with a proposed $3 million undertaking, the Ohio and Pennsylvania governments each found itself in bitter disputes. First, the canal would drastically hurt business for nearby Fairport and Ashtabula Harbor.

The gateway to Lake Erie had the canal way been built. *Author's collection*

Both harbors acted as huge moneymakers for the State of Ohio. Next, folks worried that the canal would disrupt many natural waterways in both states. Some even feared that the canal would slowly drain Lake Erie.

After fifty years of litigation, the Lake Erie and Pittsburgh Canal never materialized. Eventually, investors gave up on the idea and moved on to other projects. The United States government vetoed the idea in 1951 once and for all. Had the canal project succeeded, GOTL would have taken on a completely different personality.

Indian Creek Shipping

Indian Creek, located on the eastern end of town, has always played an important role in the growth of GOTL. So named for the legend of a Native American, Little John, Indian Creek is the center of a thriving campground today. However, long before campers flocked to the creek that empties into Lake Erie, several industrial proprietors made use of the natural flow of the creek.

In the 1820s, colonist George Turner and his wife settled on the creek and established a sawmill. The mill was initially powered by water but was later converted to steam. Turner soon needed a way to transport his lumber to nearby Ashtabula Harbor. So, with a little help, Turner built the first of many boats constructed at Indian Creek.

In addition to milling lumber and building boats, there arose a need for methods of loading boats. Fortunately, about two miles west, a little business had been started by Fitch and Spencer, who created barrel staves with some of their lumber. More than likely, business transactions occurred between the companies. Regardless, Indian Creek became a staple in the community not only for lumber but also, interestingly, for boat construction.

At the mouth of this small creek, numerous shallow-draft vessels were built and launched directly into the lake. The shipbuilding was headed by a gentleman named Perry White, who oversaw many boats built and launched from the creek. The boats had to be constructed for shallow water, as the lakeshore is sprinkled with sandbars that can wreak havoc on boats. Eventually, the men decided to build the largest boat of its time.

The large scow, named the *Vampire*, was to be launched from the Indian Creek boatyard in 1867. As news spread of the completion of the *Vampire*, the townspeople awaited the day of its launching. Soon all was readied for takeoff. A large crowd gathered and was quite fascinated by the huge beast. The proud sailors hopped aboard, and it was launched into the fast-moving water of Indian Creek. Oh the majesty of such a grand boat as it approached the turquoise water! What great adventures must lie ahead for it!

However, the *Vampire* was not to be so easily led out to sea. Instead, once the huge vessel entered Lake Erie, there arose a loud *thunk*, followed by a dragging noise. The crowd must have been quite excited at this point, for the people quickly realized that the much talked-about *Vampire* was indeed stuck in the shallow waters of Lake Erie.

Apparently, the ship was too heavy, even though precautions had been taken beforehand. Shipyard workers thus spent the day in front of the crowd shoveling sand from under the vessel. Eventually, the *Vampire* was relaunched and sent on its way to Ashtabula Harbor for another fitting. This fiasco would be one of the last attempts to build and launch large boats from Indian Creek.

The Legend of Indian Creek

Coming to town nowadays, visitors will quickly learn of the beautiful campground that sits in the far eastern part of the town. The successful camping resort, known as Indian Creek, is rich in GOTL history and sprinkled with a speckling of town folklore.

About two miles east of the current state lodge, a small stream flows into the lake. The peaceful little stream, Indian Creek, is so named because it has been passed down that the banks once held the grave of a Native American. The story of the grave and the person buried there has circulated for more than two centuries.

Legend has it that a Chippewa Indian (English name Little John) and his wife and children had constructed a wigwam at the mouth of the creek. Along with a few other natives, the group was in the area on a hunting and fishing expedition. The closest white inhabitants were located in Harpersfield, about eight miles away.

One late evening in 1806, a couple of Chippewa Indians approached the house of Major Morse in Harpersfield. Although the natives spoke no English, it was very apparent from their mannerisms that something was wrong. For one, the Indians had painted themselves in black. Also, the look of grief in their eyes was unmistakable. Morse and his family realized that they were being asked to accompany the natives back to the little creek.

Apparently, the very beloved Little John has suffered a fatal accident. While chopping down a tree for game, Little John was killed by the falling timber. The natives expressed great grief and shock, which was not typically their custom. It was accepted by this particular group that death was a part of life and that one simply passed to another world. However, the white men quickly understood that the natives wanted them to feel their pain concerning Little John's passing. The white men were made to understand

Indian Creek in 1908 was considerably wider than today. Thus, large vessels would have been able to navigate the large creek bed. *Author's collection.*

that "they had called for them to be witnesses of their misfortune and to assist at the funeral of their dearest friend."

Little John's body was buried according to custom, in a sitting posture, with his knife, hatchet, kettle and rifle beside him. The grave itself, located on the western bank of the creek, was marked by a red painted post completely enclosed by several tall posts. Unfortunately, the burial site was later robbed by thieves, who took artifacts and even Little John's remains. Thus, local ghost stories about Little John's soul arose and continue today.

SCHOOL IS IN SESSION

By the 1830s, the population of the tiny town of GOTL was primarily made up of young families. Thus, it became necessary, due to the number of children in the area, to construct a schoolhouse. Reuben Warner was instrumental in the development of the school. By 1838, the town had its first wooden, one-room schoolhouse located on the eastern end of town. Children would follow along the lake as they made their way to the little school on days they were not needed on the farm.

Geneva Township School as it appeared in 1961. *Cleveland Press Collection, courtesy of CSU Michael Schwartz Library, Special Collections.*

In 1883, the school was rebuilt using brick. The school operated for twenty-five more years, until 1909. Students from the little school and Cowles Creek School were consolidated to a new centralized school in Geneva. School board records have been lost for the most part. However, area researchers have found accounts in journals about a young female teacher of the school in the early 1900s. In her writings, along with the daily trials of early education, the teacher often mentions the sound of the lake nearby. She seemed to fear that the lake was ready to claim the banks and everything on it, including the schoolhouse. The teacher also mentioned the need for more lighting due to the thickness of the trees that surrounded the building.

The little school remains today in the middle of Geneva Township Park. At one point, the park's caretaker resided in the building, and it also once housed a town office. Nowadays, the building is considered a historical landmark, and a committee was formed in order to continuously preserve the school and township park.

CHAPTER 2

RESORT BEGINNINGS

S oon after the close of the Civil War, the town noted the presence of weary travelers, mostly soldiers on their way home from a hard-fought war. Around this time, the Fitch family, who had built a second house in 1824 on their land, opened doors to transit travelers. The boardinghouse, which was the first frame house in the area, is now known as the Jennie Munger Gregory Museum.

Not only did the boardinghouse host many weary soldiers, but it also was a stopover for early settlers of the Western Reserve. While staying at the boardinghouse, guests observed the busy woodcutting industry of Fitch's Landing.

In 1906, the Fitch family sold the property to the Gregory family, who were part of the first generation of GOTL settlers. Later, after her husband's untimely death, Jennie Munger Greogory used the home as her summer residence and lived in the town of Geneva in the winter months. Upon her death, the home was willed to the Ashtabula Historical Society as long as it would keep the name of Jennie Munger Gregory. In 1962, the society held a grand opening and set up headquarters in the large house.

Today, visitors are invited to view relics from the boarding years. Antique furniture, fashions and books from Ashtabula County's past are showcased throughout the nine rooms. Researchers have access to numerous archives concerning county history.

Another town resident who capitalized on the town's growing popularity was Cullen Spencer, Harvey's son. Harvey maintained ownership of his

The Jennie Munger Gregory House in 1961. The next year, the home would be willed to the Ashtabula Historical Society. *Cleveland Press Collection, courtesy of CSU Michael Schwartz Library, Special Collections.*

original farmland, Sturgeon Point, until his later years. In 1870, Cullen gained the property deed and continued to expand on an idea that launched the town into what it is today.

RESORT OF SORTS

As the United States settled down from the upheaval of wars, boundary disputes and settlement transitions, people began to seek a little rest and relaxation. Word spread in the Ohio and Pennsylvania areas about a cozy little village on the banks of Lake Erie. This village was marked by long sandy beaches, cool lake breezes and a fishing hole completely stocked with an assortment of species. As hardworking families toiled along in their new lives, a getaway as such sounded quite appealing. Thus, the little village experienced an influx of campers seeking all the pleasures that the lake had to offer. Families happily pitched their tents in the woodsy areas or directly on the beaches, not knowing that they were the original vacationers of Ohio's first resort.

Meanwhile, Cullen Spencer and his friend, Edward Pratt, took note of this new vacationing trend in their little village. Being lake lovers themselves,

A young boy poses in front of a "Geneva Park" billboard. Land at the "finest summer resort" was advertised for $750 per lot. *Author's collection.*

the gentlemen wished to create an area for folks to take full advantage of the lovely area. Thus, in 1869, Sturgeon Point, now known as the Mapleton Beach area, was officially opened as a public picnic area, with easy beach access. In no time at all, the grounds became a popular destination, and Spencer quickly bought up neighboring land to expand on his project. Four years later, the partners added a horse-powered merry-go-round. Thus, a town known for beaches, camping, amusements and great family activities was born.

VACATIONERS ARRIVE

In the later years of the 1800s, a national phenomenon in transportation took place that brought more visitors to the town. As railway construction boomed in the mid-1800s, Ohio was eyed as an ideal location to run branches of line. Not only did the state have huge manufacturing cities, but it also had access to a Great Lake.

Furthering Ohio railway development was the fact that the state was located between several national cities. By 1890, Ohio was an enormous entanglement of rail lines heading north, south, east and west.

Originally, the focus of the Ohio lines was the transportation of cargo to and from industries. Early passenger travel was thought to be quite dangerous, as many mishaps occurred along the rails. However, with the invention of the T-rail, stronger steel rails and ballast rock used to strengthen the line, railway tycoons realized that train travel was just on the horizon, according to John King on american-rails.com: "With the foundation of equipment introduced by 1850 for early passenger trains, and the industry as a whole, new and better technologies helped make traveling by rail more comfortable, efficient, and faster. These included specialized cars like diners, sleepers, club cars, parlor cars, and observations."

Thus, passenger trains were now ready to carry travelers from town to town in what was considered a timely fashion in the early years. In the late 1800s to mid-1900s, railways would reach their "golden years."

EARLY VACATIONERS

Campers continued to visit the town, laying tents all about. How peaceful it must have been to see the many campfires lit up and down the shoreline. Families huddled together, with only the sound of the waves and laughter as background music. Up on the bluffs, tucked back safely in the woods, a few small cabins and farmhouses could be seen as their night candles flickered in the darkness.

The Rose Cottage, GOTL's first summer boardinghouse. The large house is still standing and houses several gift shops. *Author's collection.*

Sturgeon Point Boarding House was built on Cullen Spencer's land, Mapleton Beach area. *Author's collection.*

In the year 1869, it is interesting to note that only five structured houses existed along the modern-day strip. Solomon Fitch, Cullen Spencer and a few others had established boardinghouses for wayward travels. But it would be W.E. Spencer who would be the first to open a summer vacation house, known as Rose Cottage.

By 1905, nearly fifty-three cottages held summer boarders.

ROAD CONSTRUCTION AHEAD

Lake Erie's formative era established many of the current lake-area roads. At the end of the glaciation period, the glaciers receded northward, leaving beach ridges and flat lake plains as they went. These ridges would one day become the well-worn trails and paths created by the natives. As the settlers migrated to the area, they would also utilize the trails on the ridges. Today, State Route 20 is sometimes referred to as the north ridge path, while State Route 84 is known as the south ridge path.

Likewise, State Route 531 was formed by natural boundaries set by the lake. Natives of the area utilized this trail as a lake access path and as a hunting trail. Moses Cleaveland and his party most likely utilized the trail as they surveyed the area. As the new families settled in, their horses and buckboards continued to wear the path down. Thus, Lake Road was essentially formed by early people utilizing the lake.

LAKE ROAD MOVED

As settlers moved in, the path widened into a dirt road. The dirt path was located quite close to the bluffs, allowing for easy access to the lake. Homes in the early days included huge lawns that stretched to the lake road and then on to the lake. Thus, some of the older homes of today have front doors that used to be the back doors in earlier times.

Above: An early postcard of the dirt road leading to GOTL. *Author's collection.*

Below: The original Lake Shore Boulevard dead-ends at Geneva Township Park. *Author's collection.*

With more traffic rolling through town, and the ever-hungry lake eating away at the shores, Lake Shore Boulevard, as it was named at the time, needed to be reconstructed farther from the lake. In 1912, part of the road was moved one block south, creating the present-day strip. Evidence of the original road can be found at the west entrance to Geneva's Township Park, where Old Lake Road dead-ends. Much of the former Lake Shore Boulevard is underwater now.

In the early 1920s, the Geneva and Lake Erie Automobile Line brought visitors to the lakeshore. In Geneva, travelers could board the car from the train station. The ride through Geneva was quite pleasant, as a brick-paved road had been laid through town. However, once the car passed the Water Street intersection, the pavement stopped. From there on out, travelers reported that it was time to "hang on to your hats" as they rode along the deeply rutted road into GOTL.

CHAPTER 3

EARLY INNS AND BOARDINGHOUSES

O ver the next few decades, GOTL continued to see the construction of new hotels, boardinghouses and inns. Dozens of rentals lined the main road from the intersection of 534 to the eastern end of the town boundaries. From grand inns to huge boardinghouses, GOTL offered much in the way of overnight accommodations. From an American Plan, which included three meals at a quoted price, to a European Plan, which meant getting meals on your own, guests were treated to luxurious retreats. Several of the ritzy inns took guests by referral only, and Shady Beach only allowed white guests of European descent. They continued this policy well into the late 1950s. Most people in the early portion of the twentieth century were well-to-do families. During summer months, the *Cleveland Plain Dealer* included lists of where the city's wealthiest vacationed.

Nelson Warner, of Warner's Hotel Colonial and also a founding father of the township, reportedly ran a surrey and team to the nearby Geneva railroad station to pick up vacationers. These boarders, mainly from the Pittsburgh area, would hop on the surrey with quite a bit of luggage. After all, many guests planned to stay for the entire summer. As they pulled into the Warner Hotel, Mrs. Warner would be on the porch to greet the guests and offer them a glass of lemonade after a long journey. After getting the guest settled in, she would go back to the business of running a fully functioning hotel. She would spend the summer preparing meals, cleaning rooms and making guests feel right at home.

By the early 1900s, GOTL was well underway as a favorite resort destination. Families who could afford it rented rooms from the inns along

HOTEL SHADY BEACH

Above: Brochure cover for Shady Beach Hotel and Cottages. The ad inside reads: "Shady Beach beckons you to enjoy its far-famed hospitality and its unequaled location on Lake Erie. Socially discriminating clientele." *Author's collection.*

Below: The expansive lawn at Ramsey's Inn. Lawns such as this were quite common during the early resort years. *Author's collection.*

the sandy lakeshore. At the time, guests enjoyed all the pleasures that the lake had to offer. Activities included pleasant picnics on the bluff, swimming in the frothy waves, building sand castles and waiting patiently for a bite on the fishing line. Baseball games were scheduled between popular boardinghouses. Back at the inns, families enjoyed simply lounging on the enormous wraparound porches, a card game on the patio, a stroll down the lane and, of course, eating many delicious meals.

Meanwhile, other trends along the lake were beginning to take hold. Picnic grounds, campgrounds and private groves were emerging and quickly

GENEVA ON THE LAKE
GENEVA, OHIO

Spend Sunday and Labor Day Here

An Ideal Place to Spend a Vacation in the Month of September. MAKE RESERVATIONS.

Idle-a-While	The New Inn	Forget-Me-Not Cottage
Sidney Ramsey	Swan & Swan	Rufus M. Hoskins
Tuscar Inn	**Grand View House**	**Sturgeon Point House**
Mrs. N. A. Parker	Chas. H. Hews	T. C. Spencer
Buckeye Cottage	**The Casino**	**Wayside Cottage**
Clarence Hoskins	Dancing Pavilion	Wm. French
Four Gables	**Colonial Cottage**	**Rose Cottage**
Homer Cadmus	Chas. H. Warner	Walter Ross

Above: An advertisement for various inns and boardinghouses in 1925, *Star Beacon Journal*, Ashtabula, Ohio.

Below: Buckeye Beach area in 1910. *Columbus Metropolitan Library Digital Collection.*

expanding. Quaint yet classy names were given to certain areas of the town. This included Buckeye Beach, Mapleton Beach and Warner's Landing.

Popular lodgings at the time included the Leidheiser Hotel, Idle-a-While, Warren Spencer's, Rose Cottage, Cullen Spencer's Sturgeon Point, Rufus Hoskin's Forget Me Not, Old Orchard Home, The Homestead, Warner's Colonial Inn, Bert Warner's Eagle Cliff and Shady Beach Inn.

Above: Front lawn at Ramsey's Idle-a-While Cottage, one of the most prestigious inns of the time. Sturgeon Point Condominiums replaced the once fabulous cottage. *Author's collection.*

Below: Gregory's Four Gables. *John D. "Jack" Sargent Geneva on the Lake Collection.*

Traditionally, on the last weekend of the season, Labor Day weekend, most inns would present a show, known as a frolic. For example, in 1920, the Forget Me Not staged a comedic mock wedding. The show began at the inn, proceeded to the Bird Cage and Casino and then ended with the "wedding ceremony" on the beach. Shows and silly performances such as these were favorite traditions for most guests and ended seasons on a high note.

Another elaborate inn of the time was the Gregory's Four Gables. Not only did it offer fine dining and luxurious living quarters, but it also offered a huge bathing house right on the beach. At one point, the Gregory's Beach area had an extremely long slide that ran from the top of the bluff straight into the lake. Later the slide was lost to fire.

OTHER BOARDINGHOUSES AND INNS

All over town, boardinghouse and inns continued to appear, with each seemingly fancier than the last.

Above: The Welcome. *Author's collection.*

Left: Tuscar Inn. *Author's collection.*

CHAPTER 4

RESORT LIFE

W ord of the little resort spread throughout Ohio and Pennsylvania. Advertisements for lodgings appeared in newspapers in both states. There was just something about this area, even back then, that seemed to guarantee a peaceful and enjoyable summer day. Families could not resist the small beach town charm that offered cool breezes just far enough away from the hustle and bustle of city life.

Three such guests felt that the lore of the lake could be found quietly fishing along the shore. Henry Ford, John D. Rockefeller and Harvey Firestone frequented the area on numerous camping trips. The three gentlemen—who were collectively responsible for the development of the automobile, which in turn helped GOTL flourish—found the area to be a favorite spot. Rockefeller, the world's first billionaire, could have easily traveled anywhere in the world. Yet just like thousands of folks today, he must have realized that there was just something about this resort.

As John D. Rockefeller said, "Don't be afraid to give up the good things to go for the great."

TAKING CARE OF BUSINESS

With the newfound vacation industry, it seemed only natural for tourist-related businesses to emerge. Folks were delighted to swim and play on the beach, yet what would happen if more entertainment facilitates and eateries were to emerge?

After all, all over Ohio, amusement parks such as Euclid Beach, Chippewa Lake and Buckeye Lake were steadily on the rise to fame as family destinations.

In 1914, the first sandwich stand opened on the corner of Lake Road and North Spencer Drive. Later, the business was sold, and the New Inn opened there. The Warners' huge expanse of property eventually turned into the heart of the business district, with much of it being donated by the Warners themselves.

The New Inn quickly turned a new profit. The inn was not only a boarder's dream but also a restaurant of sorts. Sunday nights, in particular, offered huge home-cooked meals, and it was not unusual for hundreds of guests to show. The New Inn advertised chicken dinners made with only milk-fed chickens. However, the former owner, Mrs. Swan, was later quoted as saying that "those chickens never saw a drop of milk."

The New Inn also served as the town's first post office, opening in 1915. GOTL residents petitioned to have a post office, especially for their summer

The Homestead, another Warner family boardinghouse. Later, Tomas "Uncle Tom" Kainaroi bought the house from Reuben Warner's granddaughter and converted it to a family summer home and office for his cottage business. *Cleveland Press Collection, courtesy of CSU Michael Schwartz Library, Special Collections.*

Above: The New Inn was known for home-cooked meals and advertised on the front sign. *Columbus Metropolitan Library Digital Collection.*

Below: The New Inn in later years was converted to the Swiss Chalet. Note in the far right of the picture the small post office that served GOTL for almost fifty years. *Author's collection.*

visitors. Mrs. Swan would arrive at the Geneva Depot at 6:00 a.m. sharp to retrieve the mail from the early morning train. The New Inn acted as a summer post office until 1964.

Above: The Casino ballroom hosted many exquisite dances. Later, the building would become a skating rink. In 1979, the dance hall burned to the ground. *Author's collection.*

Below: Inside view of the Casino. Other dance halls of the day included the Birdcage and Pergola Dance Gardens. *Author's collection.*

Also in 1914, Bert and Jenny Gregory built the Casino dance hall, located west of the New Inn. The Gregorys sold the Casino to Glick and Johnson just two years later. Glick and Johnson established a quality dance hall there.

Shorts were never allowed, and gentlemen were expected to wear ties. Friday nights were "dress up" nights, and only the best fashions of the time were expected to be seen on the dance floor.

THE NEW ENTREPRENEURS

Just as the Spencer family is credited with the early growth of the resort, another family with an eye for business and a love for entertainment earned credit for the growth of the amusement side of the resort.

In the early 1920s, a young couple by the name of Eusebio and Martha Pera decided to visit the much-talked-about Geneva on the Lake. They had heard that there was land for sale here. And besides that, the Geneva name reminded Mrs. Pera of her home in Switzerland. Living and working in Cleveland at the time, the town was just down the lake a couple hours. As the couple traveled along the lake, they must have discussed their own little business in Cleveland, where they owned and operated a restaurant.

Before coming to Ohio, Eusebio had worked at the New York Waldorf-Astoria hotel and at a resort hotel in Florida. Therefore, when they arrived at GOTL, the two were quite impressed with the flourishing tourist resort. Eusebio reportedly fell in love with the quaint little place and quickly made plans to move the family to the area.

The New Inn's lawns eventually become Pera's Park and Kiddie Land. Erieview Park grew from this small recreation area. *Author's collection.*

The New Inn always had a crowd of vacationers. *Author's collection.*

In 1921, the Peras sold their business in Cleveland and returned to GOTL with a new business offer in hand. The Peras purchased the twenty-two-room New Inn and soon added on to the already popular hotel. A tennis court and a small recreation area behind the hotel called "Pera's Park," with beach access, were developed. This little recreation area would eventually become a favorite amusement park for generations to come.

BEGINNING OF FUN

As the Peras worked side by side (as Pera and Pera, no less), the air was filled with excitement. In the 1920s, the Peras commissioned the building of a grand ballroom unlike any other from Cleveland to New York. The Pier Ballroom was marked by an airy and spacious dance area, a crystal ball and the most popular big bands of the day.

The Day the Music Almost Stopped

In August 1935, the Pier Ballroom proudly presented Tommy Tucker and his orchestra. Each night, crowds gathered to listen to the very popular band

Above: The Pier Ballroom was one of the most popular ballrooms in Ohio. Many big bands of the day were honored to be invited to play at the Pier. *John D. "Jack" Sargent Geneva on the Lake Collection.*

Below: In nearby Geneva, visitors to Ree's Drug Store can view Mr. Ree's collection of posters from the Pier. Mr. Ree worked at the Pier as a rope boy and frequently brought the advertisements home. *Author's collection.*

play the night away. However, one afternoon, as Tommy prepared for the big show, he noticed that all the music books, papers and notes were nowhere to be found. He quickly called for the Peras. Upon further inspection, they

An interior room depicted on a Shady Beach brochure. *Author's collection.*

realized that a window had been broken in the back of the ballroom. The thief had made off with all the musical documents. The estimated loss for the music and the window was about $15,000. The music would be worth quite a bit more if recovered today. Tommy and his orchestra knew that the show had to go on and were able to play from memory. The music and thief were never located.

Kay Kyiser also spent much time at the Pier. In his early days, before fame, Kay would camp out in the attic of Shady Beach. The owners, the Bowers, would allow Kay to stay for the entire summer for just cents per day. As Kay became more famous, he returned to the inn with his entire entourage. The group would rent out many of the suites from the Bowers at the stated rental fee.

OTHER FUN

Another young entrepreneur focused his attention on the one timeless attraction: Lake Erie itself. In 1914, Clarence Hoskins, owner of the Buckeye Hotel, operated his fast boat for guests. The trip, known as pleasure boating, could be rented for fishing and sightseeing. In 1920, the boat was replaced by a new Red Wing and advertised "a gulls eye view" of the shoreline.

Throughout town, added amusements were appearing. The Shady Beach hotel constructed a fantastic tennis court, a picture gallery, a sandwich shop, a one-lane bowling alley and its own private dance hall. Shady Beach also advertised a grand Sunday dinner to the town if the inn was not too busy.

Hoskins's Red Wing, loaded with guests of the Buckeye Beach Hotel. *John D. "Jack" Sargent Geneva on the Lake Collection.*

MINIATURE GOLF

In the early 1920s, the miniature golf craze was sweeping the nation. As GOTL proprietors wished to provide more attractions for visitors, the resort was not to be left out on the new game. Thus, in 1924, the first mini-golf course was constructed and opened in GOTL. Today known as Allison's Miniature Golf, the course is believed to be the oldest course in continuous play in the United States.

However, times were not always easy in the miniature golf industry. During the 1930s, the mini-golf craze took a nosedive. Only resorts and other amusement industries were able to profit from the game. Fortunately, in the late 1940s, the mini-golf or putt-putt industry became in full swing once again.

GOLF

Entertainment businesses continued to emerge throughout the late 1920s. In 1926, GOTL opened a state-of-the-art nine-hole golf course. By 1954, the course had expanded into the traditional eighteen-hole game. The course is considered today by golf enthusiasts to be one of the best in northeast Ohio, especially after the $1 million renovations in the 1990s.

Trouble on the Golf Course

On a hot summer afternoon in 1935, the town constable was in hot pursuit of a crook in the area. The wild goose chase had led the constable to the golf course. Being quite an open area, it was not long before the criminal was apprehended. After cuffing the man, the constable began to lead his catch off the course. However, out from behind a nearby tree sprang two other rough-looking guys. In order to save their leader, the man in custody, they had to wrestle the constable to the ground. The three men then sped back across the course. By this time, everyone on the course was aware of the problem and assisted the constable. Soon, all three men were caught and taken to Mayor Warner for their sentencing. Warner, who was known for his fairness, determined that the men were flat broke. They were unable to pay their twenty-dollar fine. The mayor ordered that the three men should work off their debt on the golf course for the remainder of the week.

As the ballrooms and golf courses emerged, drawing more folks to the lakeside, other small concessions begin to appear throughout the town. A town directory from 1932 lists several eateries and game stands, mainly concentrated toward the midway area (from the Jim Lavender Collection):

Sohio Gas Station	Standard Drug Company
Zimmerman Ice Station	Original Bike Shop
Hyde Barber & Beauty Shop	Frozen Dessert
Geneva Sportland	Bingo Parlor
Casino	Shooting Gallery
Cocktail Bar	Archery
Post Office	Pitch & Putt Golf Courses
Gulf Gas Station	Popcorn Ball
Miller Reality	Picture Shop
Lake Shore Gardens	Carlisle-Allen Resort Shop
Shupp & Shupp Bicycles	Cottage Restaurant
The Pier	Erie Shore's Ice Cream
Times Square	Eddie Stewart's Sandwich Shop
Erie Grill	Stewart's Restaurant
19th Hole	Golf Driving Range
Shupp Drug Company	

CHAPTER 5

OUR TOWN

Today, vacationers in the area tend to forget that although GOTL is a favorite resort destination, the town still must function as, well, a town. Throughout the year, a busy town council, fire department, police department and various committees continue to toil away with or without summer tourists. According to the 2009 census, 1,490 people are year-round residents of the town. Just as summer vacationers return to their hometowns to mow the lawn and pay taxes, the residents of GOTL continue to function as a town long after the last ice cream cone is devoured by a summer vacationer.

ELECTRIC AND SEWER: A LUXURY

In 1919, Geneva on the Lake received the luxury of electricity. In 1927, the town was fully incorporated and offered plans for a city sewer. Many of the successful hotels and businesses at the time signed up to be located on the town water and sewer line. Having such accommodations was considered a luxury at the time. If an establishment had such a novelty, it was sure to advertise "hot showers" and "modern bath accommodations."

FIRE DEPARTMENT

Like many other small towns in the early twentieth century, GOTL did not have an official fire department. In fact, when a fire would start, townspeople would organize and use the old bucket brigade system.

Due to the town's growing population and ongoing construction of large hotel-like buildings, the little community realized that the current firefighting system would not suffice in major emergencies. In 1924, several gentlemen, all business owners, petitioned the State of Ohio for authority to create a fire district. Eusebio Pera, Charles Warner, Emery Tyler, Clearance Hoskins, Charles Craine, Arthur Bowers, Durwood Bowers and Sidney Ramsey became the founding fathers and the first firemen of the Geneva on the Lake Fire Department.

In 1925, the newly formed department put in an order for a Graham Brothers fire truck, which the firemen bought themselves. The fire truck was a four-cylinder, open-cab model. In the event of an emergency, the truck had a hand-operated siren to clear traffic and two soda-acid chemical tanks to put out a blaze. For years, the truck proved its worth as it rushed from fire to fire. Later, after its retirement, the truck was displayed in town parades and won many prizes.

One initial problem for the department was the question of where to house the brand-new truck. Emery Tyler, who owned and operated the Rose Cottage, offered an old barn sitting on his property. The other gentlemen were very delighted with this offer and soon made Mr. Tyler the first acting fire chief. The little barn housed the department until 1970.

In 1987, business entrepreneurs Don Woodward, Dave Otto and Joyce Otto were busily making plans to open a new winery. As they walked over some of the Woodward property, they stopped in front of an old barn with a rusty old fire truck parked out front. Within moments, the new winery's location was decided.

Today, the Old Firehouse Winery proudly displays the 1924 Graham Brothers truck. While visitors sip wine and buy tickets for the Ferris wheel, they may linger in the little building and enjoy original firehouse memorabilia placed artistically throughout the business.

POLICE DEPARTMENT

As the resort's popularity grew, so did the need for law enforcement. In 1927, a town constable was appointed to oversee the summer crowd and the 114 year-round residents. In 1980, a full-time police department was added. Over the years, the department has struggled with the most efficient way to deal with the crowds. Hence, in the 1970s, officers on horseback were seen patrolling the strip. In the 1990s, visitors were quite fascinated with the policemen riding on state-of-the-art mountain bikes. In recent years, traditional police cruisers, some with K-9 units, have been seen policing the streets.

MAYOR

Charlie Warner, grandson of Reuben Warner, is credited with developing the township's political life. He was very instrumental in bringing water and sewer, as well as the golf course, to the town. He pushed for the incorporation of the village. In 1928, Charlie became the first mayor of the village.

In 1930, Charlie's son, Howard, was elected mayor. Howard had completed a law degree at Case Western Reserve University. State newspapers picked up on his story and ran articles about Ohio's youngest mayor. Charlie was twenty-five when he took on the leadership role.

In 1910, Township Park was established. The public was always invited to use the beach on the grounds of the park. *Author's collection.*

CHAPTER 6

SURVIVING

As GOTL began to settle into a peaceful routine of catering to summer vacationers in the late 1920s, a turbulent time for the country was beginning to take stage. In 1929, the country experienced the stock market crash, which propelled the world into the worst economic depression in its history. Families experienced the harshest forms of poverty up to that date.

PARK PLAN DANCING

As small businesses collapsed all over the country, the young proprietors of GOTL sought methods to stay afloat during this dark period. The Pier Ballroom adopted a "park plan" dancing system. Dancers were required to pay a ten-cent fee per dance. Once the tune ended, the rope boys swept across the floor. Each boy held one end of a rope that stretched from one side of the dance floor to the other. Starting on a far end of the floor, the boys walked the rope down the dance floor, sweeping off the guests. Once the floor was cleared, a collection was taken for the next dance. Once that song ended, the rope boys' work started over again.

Another more infamous example of capital gain occurred at the Pergola Dance Gardens. The Pergola was a popular arena with a spacious dancing area. This new method for making a buck while entertaining the downtrodden was sweeping the nation. Dance marathons, sometimes called walk marathons or human endurance contests, were quickly becoming a form of business industry.

Dance contestants would enter the marathon with their eyes on a monetary prize. Contestants from the local villages as well as professional dancers attempted to outlast one another. These contests could extend from hours to several days. The goal was to keep dancing upright without allowing a knee to hit the floor.

Hundreds of visitors from the local towns gathered to be entertained. Carol Martin, author of *Dance Marathons: Performing American Culture in the 1920s and 1930s*, described the audience members as "unemployed, bored, and sometimes angry, spectators [who] spent days and nights watching the 'kids' make endless rounds on the dance floor."

After paying a cover charge to enter, spectators could cheer, make bets and even converse directly with the couples in the contest. This, in turn, encouraged the dancers to keep dancing.

In order to distract from the monotony of the marathon, a lively announcer, or master of ceremony, promoted other spectacular events to amaze the audience. Local performers and sometimes hired actors conducted amazing acts on the dance floor. With performances by local burlesque girls, dancing clowns, magicians, comedians, boxers and even surprise visits from celebrities, the shows included a variety of excitements in order to keep guests entertained and returning day after day, paying the cover charge each time.

But nothing compared to the thrill of watching the marathoners not just dance but also perform ordinary tasks such as shaving, eating and brushing their teeth while they moved. These tasks proved to be quite humorous and allowed for the audience to connect with the dancers on a personal level. The real climax of the show, however, were the moments when couples would begin to drop out of the contest, either by collapsing, falling asleep or walking off the floor. As the last two couples vied it out, the audience would cheer in anticipation for the second-best couple to drop out, revealing the new reigning champs.

Dance Record Set at GOTL

On a warm spring night 1933, hundreds gathered in a huge circus-like tent pitched in the middle of GOTL. Although dance marathons were frequently conducted at the Pergola Dance Gardens, this dance had been promoted for weeks as a real humdinger of a marathon. Dance marathon celebrities would be dancing against several local couples. The promoters also promised sideshows of breathtaking proportions.

On the get-ready mark, thirty-eight couples lined the makeshift floor. With the sound of a horn, the marathon began and lasted for weeks—the audience was entertained like never before. To further add to the excitement, after eighty-seven hours, one relentless Geneva girl, Helen Natko, was left holding her own against professional dancers. Sadly, Natko received news after a week of dancing that her father had passed away. Natko chose to stay in the contest in order to win the cash prize that her family would so desperately need given her father's death.

However, the real showstopper, according to the media, was twenty-one-year-old Jimmy Parker. A professional from Chicago, his goal was to break the established world record of 142 hours for single dancers. The crowd watched Jimmy for days, struggling in pain and exhaustion. At the 169th hour, Jimmy finally set a new record. His victory dance included a quick run down the hillside and a dip into the very chilly Lake Erie.

World War II

As America entered World War II, the little town of Geneva on the Lake showed its support the only way it knew how. Although there was heavy rationing at the time, businesses and homeowners offered traveling young soldiers food, drink and board. For many, these would be the last moments of pleasure before entering the battlefield on the other side of the world.

Just as in every other small town, GOTL residents waited relentlessly for word to come that this dreadful and deadly war had ended. Hours were spent by the family radio listening to the president make speeches that things were getting better—only to wait some more for an official end. Tin drives and victory gardens were part of daily life. Conservation of resources was standard living at the time.

As for the resort life at the time, the tourist industry slowed. However, many folks found work in Ohio at nearby defense plants. Therefore, people did remain employed at the time, bringing just enough business to the resort to keep it afloat.

Finally, on one hot evening in August 1945, word spread throughout the town. Japan had surrendered to the Allied forces, bringing the war to an end. This would forever mark August 14, 1945, as V-D day. As

A gentleman enjoys a day on the beach at GOTL. In 1940, his suit was in vogue with men's fashions. *Author's collection.*

news traveled, folks in Geneva on the Lake entered the streets shouting and banging pots and pans. What a celebration! Hugging and cheering continued throughout the day as the news became a reality.

At the close of the war, American families experienced a newfound economic peacefulness. Industries in the nation were much in need of workers, and the economy in general was on the upswing. With this comfortable new lifestyle, families were able to afford vehicles, homes, food and even vacations. Families in the next few years would expand in size, ushering in the baby boom years immediately following the war. Thus, with money in pocket and little ones in tow, families would infiltrate areas such as GOTL looking for some fun and relaxation. The next few decades would go down in history as GOTL's heyday as a popular resort.

LET THE GOOD TIMES ROLL

Around the turn of the century, visitors to the resort were mainly arriving from nearby areas. Train travel was available, but tickets were quite pricey, especially for families. Still, something huge was happening in an industrious city on Lake Michigan. After successfully constructing and selling a few high-tech contraptions known as vehicles, Henry Ford was now prepared to mass-produce his product. Although the invention of car-like machines had been taking place all over the world, it would be Ford who would introduce the first made-for-family transportation. The Model T, recently named the car of the twentieth century, would be the mode of transportation that would launch family vacations for years to come. Henry Ford was quoted as saying:

> *I will build a car for the great multitude. It will be large enough for the family, but small enough for the individual to run and care for. It will be constructed of the best materials, by the best men to be hired, after the simplest designs that modern engineering can devise. But it will be so low in price that no man making a good salary will be unable to own one—and enjoy with his family the blessing of hours of pleasure in God's great open spaces.*

With the accessibility of mobility, more and more guests from Cleveland, Akron, Youngstown and Pittsburgh began making their way to the cozy little lakeside town. These folks desired to escape the oppressiveness of the stifling city air and the hot, dank factories where many were employed.

The popularity of the automobile sparked another event that further developed family travel. As hundreds and then thousands of vehicles chugged their way across the United States, road conditions became a major concern in government projects. Old stagecoach paths became state routes. Route 20, which runs parallel to the lake, eventually became the longest highway in the country, crossing twelve states from east to west. Relics of the stagecoach days, including inns and boardinghouses, can still be found today along the Ohio portion of the road.

CHAPTER 7

FAMILY STYLE

With a change in family dynamics, there arose a need for a new type of accommodation for guests. In previous years, the well-to-do were able to rent a room or two in one of the boardinghouses. But as the baby boom years blossomed, families needed more room to accommodate bigger families. A brochure in 1950 boasted an astounding choice among nine hundred cottages. Many of the cabins and cottages constructed in these days are easily recognizable in current times.

UNCLE TOM'S

One of the largest cabin and motel properties along the strip is known as Uncle Tom's. Over the years, the area has grown to contain twenty-four cottages, a nine-room efficiency motel and a twelve-room apartment complex. However, this vast expanse of rental property did not expand overnight. Instead, a man with a passion for GOTL added to his "home away from home" over a period of several decades.

Tomas Kainaroi first came to visit GOTL from his hometown of Homestead, Pennsylvania, in the early 1930s. After just one visit, Tomas, who was a manager for Gulf Oil, was hooked and sought to buy some property in the area.

In July 1936, Tomas, then twenty, paid five dollars down with a five-dollar-per-month commitment to buy his first tiny cottage on Francis Drive. For several years, Tomas lived in the cottage during the summer months. During World War II, he was drafted, and the little cottage sat vacant for a time.

After the war, Tomas returned home and married Maggie in 1947. The couple spent many weekends and summers at the GOTL cabin. As time went on, Tomas continued to purchase additional property as money would allow. Many nights, the young couple slept in their car in order to rent out their cabin. The money was then saved in the hopes of acquiring more land.

Many of the guests fondly began calling Tomas "Uncle Tom." When people rented a cabin, they announced that they were staying at "Uncle Tom's."

Tomas and Maggie had planned right away for the addition of a family. However, the couple remained childless for eight years. Happily, in 1954, the couple's first child, Vula, was born. In Tomas's excitement, he decreed that with the birth of each child, he would add another rental to his property. Thus, in 1954, Tomas build the Presidential Drive cottage that now acts as an office and summer home for his family.

In 1956, Tomas acquired the former Homestead inn from Reuben Warner's great-great-grandchildren. He renovated the old boardinghouse and began renting rooms in the newly named Lakecrest Hotel.

In 1957, Tomas made his biggest purchase ever. He acquired the lakefront cottages across from his Presidential Drive cottage. The property included numerous cottages, a 231-foot stretch of beach and enough vacant land to build his new motel. The cottages were quite in need of updating, as many still contained old iceboxes. As Tomas and his family set to fixing up the cottages, they gave each little rental a lake-inspired name. These cottages still bear their original names: Sunset, Lakecrest, Lakebreeze, Longvue, Waterfall and Beachland.

In 1958, Uncle Tom's Motel was constructed as a second daughter, Harriet, was born. To commemorate her birth, Tomas saw to the construction of the Seaway Motel, the first lakefront motel in GOTL. Tenants could rent a room for twenty-one dollars per night.

A third child in 1961, Tammy, and the first boy in 1963 spurred Tomas on to purchase additional improvements to cottages and beach jetties in order to protect his sand. Tomas remained a Pennsylvania resident, but the family spent every summer at Uncle Tom's. Eventually, Vula and the other children took to overseeing the property in Tomas's older years. In 2005, Tomas passed away at age eighty-nine. His legacy as Uncle Tom continues to this day, as third- and fourth-generation Uncle Tom's guests continue to book their favorite rentals.

EUGOBODES

The large cluster of cottages on perhaps the prettiest lot in GOTL has recently received a facelift. As the new young owner begins her career as a landlord, she is very ecstatic as she works to restore the cabins to their former beauty.

The former Eugobodes Cottages were built by Virgil Bogue and his wife. Virgil is credited as one of the earliest town historians and was known for his ability to tell guests "just about anything on the town history." In 1927, the Bogues purchased the Silver Sands cottage on the western end of town. They eventually invested in land in the center of town on the lake side. The land had two small cottages on it. In 1936, the Bogues expanded the area to include seven large cottages. (It is now Abigail's Lakeside Cottages.)

Eugobodes Cottages in the 1950s. Until recently, the cottages had remained virtually the same for years. *Author's collection.*

LAVENDER'S COTTAGES

As Jim Lavender sat on a beach in Rio de Janeiro, he found his heart elsewhere. Yes, this place was beautiful. Yet his heart was thousands of miles away in the place where he had always vacationed.

In 1939, Jim's parents brought their one-year-old son to Chestnut Grove in GOTL. Every year, the family continued the tradition until 1955. Jim remembers swimming all day and eventually being allowed to go to "the center" (the strip) with his younger brother.

As a teen, Jim came back to GOTL with a few good buddies. This continued from 1956 to 1960. As Jim's career took off, he found himself commissioned to work in other countries. Thus, for the next few years, he was unable to get back to GOTL.

In 1965, with a wife and young son in tow, Jim rented a small cottage in Rawdon's Cottage complex. As he earned more vacation time over the years, the family's one-week stays turned into two weeks and then three weeks. Eventually, owner Roberta Shearson began renting her cottages by the summer in the 1980s. Jim jumped at the chance and booked his stay from the day Roberta turned on the water in April until she turned it off in October.

Still, Jim found that his heart longed for the little resort and the lake while he was away. In 1988, Jim noticed a man pounding a "For Sale" sign in the property next to Rawdon's. He expressed to the man that he might be interested in purchasing the large house and three small cottages, all built in the 1930s. The man simply pulled the stake from the ground, and the gentlemen began a business transaction.

In 1990, Jim and his family took ownership of the property and cottages just west of Rawdon's. The Lavenders worked together to maintain their new home and rentals, named Lavender's Cottages. In 2000, Jim retired from his full-time job and now gives his time to taking care of his rentals, taking part in civic affairs, visiting with neighbors and collecting classic cars to show off on the strip. His heart is now at home.

WIGLEY'S

A pleasant view on a postcard from Wigley's Cottages. *John D. "Jack" Sargent Geneva on the Lake Collection.*

In 2010, the former Wigley's Cottages were condemned and found to be safety hazards. The cottages had sat abandoned for several years, the owners choosing to sell the land to a private owner instead of being forced into foreclosure. The cottages have been demolished, and new construction is currently taking place.

OTHER COTTAGES

A GOTL brochure in the 1940s boasted "nine hundred cottages, fifty guest homes, twelve hotels, and fifteen restaurants." Accommodating all types of families became the key to success in these years. Breens Cottages, for example, advertised more than ninety cottages of various sizes in the Presidential area. After all, GOTL has often been referred to as "the blue-collar family playground." Indeed, working families were visiting the resort by the thousands. Many of the cottages built in this era remain intact today. Some cottages, like Breens, have been converted into family homes. Others have found new ownership as well as new names.

A father enjoys pushing his children down the strip on a summer day in 1964. *Cleveland Press Collection, courtesy of CSU Michael Schwartz Library, Special Collections.*

FOR THE FAMILY

STATE PARK
GAMES FOR ALL AGES
NIGHT CLUBS
SHOPPING
FISHING
NIGHTLY ENTERTAINMENT
GOLFING
SWIMMING
BOATING
HORSEBACK RIDES
CAMPING
TRACKLESS TRAIN
STATE APPROVED WATER

TO GREATER PLEASURE

Above: The front of a 1960s travel brochure. The inside advertised GOTL as "Ohio's Finest Wonderful Vacationland." *Author's collection.*

Left: An ad from the *Evening Gazette* from 1955 displays the many choices of cottages available.

One of the most recognizable cottage areas of the town. Allen Court Cottages and General Store are still thriving businesses today. *John D. "Jack" Sargent Geneva on the Lake Collection.*

PRIVATELY OWNED COTTAGES

Starting in the 1930s, it became quite popular for folks to build their own cabins in GOTL. Some of these cabins/cottages were used for family vacation homes, while others were permanent residences. Many cabins were and are still today privately owned. One private cottage in the Mapleton Beach area has found its place in the hearts of one family.

In 2007, Phyllis DelBene was utterly stunned when her daughter gifted her a huge wooden sign that read "Lorie Huldah." For this was the name of Phyllis's great-grandfather's cottage in Mapleton Beach. Yet the cottage had been sold years ago to someone outside the family. Michelle, Phyllis's daughter, quickly explained to her mom how she acquired the sign. It was the original sign from the cabin, and no, Michelle did not steal it. Instead, Michelle set up a covert operation, one that her mom knew nothing about, in order to get the sign.

The cottage, built sometime in the early 1900s, currently belongs to Eddie Sezon. He had purchased it from an elderly gentleman. Eddie was in the process of refurbishing the cottage for his daughter when Michelle contacted him with a favor. In exchange for the favor, Eddie was delighted to learn of the history of how the cottage, always known as the Lorie Huldah, came to be in GOTL.

William Quartier, Phyllis's great-grandfather, is believed to have been the original owner of the cottage. As he was a native of Youngstown, the GOTL cottage was a hop and a skip away for the factory worker and his wife and six children. Weekends and summers were spent at the vacation home that sat about one hundred feet from the lake.

However, life was not always a joyous time for the family. In 1911, Lorie Huldah, the Quartiers' fifth child, contacted spinal meningitis. The sixteen-year-old suffered for twelve days before passing away. In a bittersweet attempt to honor their daughter, the couple named the cottage the Lorie Huldah. Nearly one hundred years after her death, the sign on the front of the cottage still proclaimed her name.

Eventually, William and Sadie's grandchildren came to stay at the cottage. Memories at the beach would be passed down to their children. Phyllis recalled her mother sharing about days on the beach and fun evenings spent in the cozy Lorie Huldah.

In 1935, William passed away at the age of seventy-five. The family decided to let the cabin go. An elderly man purchased it and, amazingly, left the sign on the front door. It is believed that the man most likely knew the Quartiers. Thus, he left the sign in remembrance of the family.

In 2007, Eddie Sezon purchased the cabin. As Michelle completed some research on the cabin, she raced to GOTL. Eddie, after hearing the history, allowed Michelle and her family to tour the cabin and, of course, have the sign.

MOTELS AND LODGES

In the early '50s, America saw the emergence of the motel trend. Typically fashioned in an "I" or "L" shape, motels catered to motorists along the new

A copy of the hotel license obtained in order to operate Uncle Tom's Lakecrest Hotel during the 1957 season. *Ashtabula Historical Society, Jennie Munger Gregory Museum GOTL Files.*

The typical '50s motel style is shown in this postcard of Sand's Beach Motel. Other motels constructed in this era include the Dukane, Northwinds, Lake Erie Motel and Peras Motel. *John D. "Jack" Sargent Geneva on the Lake Collection.*

highway systems. GOTL quickly hopped onboard the motel trend as a means to serve guests.

Today, visitors can still find lodging reminiscent of the motel type. These places typically do very well businesswise, especially during the summer weekends. However, many are becoming outdated, especially in light of new construction within the town.

CHAPTER 8

CHESTNUT GROVE

*I don't think there is a place on earth that affects me as deeply as this place.
My brother and I visited last month, and when we drove in the gate,
it was as if all the air went out of me.*
—*Kathy Jones-Collins, former Chestnut Grove kid*

Driving into town on Route 534, the first place visitors will notice is the grandiose Geneva State Lodge. With its pristine white classiness and sparkling blue pools, the facility seems to fit perfectly in this corner of town. However, long before the lodge was ever conceived, families had laid claim to this particular area as their own personal "magical corner of the universe."

THE BEGINNINGS

From the late 1800s to early 1900s, the swampy acres west of the township were known as "the marsh." The notion of a resort seemed to stop at the western bend of Lake Road—not because there was a lack of interest in expanding but rather because the land near the Cowles Creek was densely forested and quite rugged. Thus, the name "the marsh" was fairly accurate. Yet even with the land's slightly less than perfect farming appeal, folks could not deny the beauty found in this little nook. Hundreds of chestnut trees lined the lakeshore, offering a peaceful, shady area to cool off in the lake breeze. In 1914, the Means family opened a small picnic area within the

Above: Tents scattered about during the early years of Chestnut Grove. *Jim Lavender GOTL Collection.*

Below: Spending the day on Cowles Creek was a popular activity for Chestnut Grove visitors. *Author's collection.*

shelter of the trees. Over the next few years, the Gregory family would maintain the grounds and allow for tent campers to stay on the property. The area provided much in the way of fishing and swimming, and word began to spread.

In 1918, the McKorkle family gained possession of "the marsh." The McKorkles, following the trend of the newly forming resort, expanded the grounds to include a bathhouse, a store, small cottages, lots for tents and an icehouse. Cowles Creek bordered the west of the grounds and Lake Erie the north. The beach area blocked the flow of the creek, forming a lake perfect for fishing and canoeing.

The ownership of Chestnut Grove changed hands on several occasions. At one point, Jones and Laughlin Steel purchased the land for a pretty penny in the hopes of becoming a forerunner in the proposed canal. However, once the canal project fell through, it quickly leased the land to the Neff family for ninety-nine years starting in 1920. In 1940, Lewis Kopp, a grownup "Grove kid," bought the 478-acre property as a legacy for his sons. The Kopp family held ownership until the final days of the campground.

Accommodations for campers varied in type. Standard tents could be pitched in the woods behind the cottages. Campers could also rent one of the camp-owned tents that had wooden floors and canvas coverings (easily stored each winter). These tents were available in several sizes, accommodating up to eight if need be. One family chose to camp in an old Greyhound bus, which was quite roomy to say the least.

Cabins near the lakefront were rented by the week. Most families rented for several weeks or the entire summer. The cabins were of one- or two-

The Chestnut Grove cabin area. *Author's collection.*

CHESTNUT GROVE PARK

GENEVA-ON-THE-LAKE, OHIO

One of the Best Private Beaches on Lake Erie

∎

COTTAGES, BOATS, CANOES AND CAMPING PRIVILEGES FOR RENT

Large Bath House . . . Good Fishing

∎

COTTAGES

	PER WEEK
FOR EIGHT PEOPLE—Three double beds, one day bed. New and modern. Hot and cold water, tub and shower. No. 42	$85.00
FOR SIX PEOPLE—Two double beds, one day bed. New and modern. Hot and Cold water, tub and shower. Nos. 41 and 43	$65.00
FOR EIGHT PEOPLE—Three double beds and two cots, large screened-in porch. No. 5	$55.00
FOR EIGHT PEOPLE—Three double beds and two cots, screened-in porch. Nos. 6, 7, 8, 9, and 11	$50.00
FOR EIGHT PEOPLE—Three double beds and two cots, screened-in porch. Nos. 3 and 4	$45.00
Above is a double cottage and can be made into one large cottage	$80.00
FOR SIX PEOPLE—Two double beds and two cots, screened-in porch. No. 1	$36.00
FOR FOUR PEOPLE—Two double beds, screened-in porch. Nos. 2 and 2½	$35.00
All of the above have city water, sinks, lavatories, gas and electricity.	
All listed below have city water, sinks, gas and electricity.	
FOR SIX PEOPLE—Two double beds and two cots, screened-in porch. Nos. 12, 13, 14, and 15	$35.00
FOR FIVE PEOPLE—Two double beds and one cot, screened-in porch. Nos. 20, 21, 28, and 29	$35.00
FOR FOUR PEOPLE—Two double beds, screened-in porch. Nos. 18 and 24½	$28.00
FOR FOUR PEOPLE—Two double beds, screened-in porch. Nos. 17, 19, 22, and 23	$24.00
FOR THREE PEOPLE—One double bed and one cot, screened-in porch. Nos. 24, 25, and 32	$22.00
FOR TWO PEOPLE—One double bed, screened-in porch. Nos. 10 and 16	$20.00
FOR TWO PEOPLE—One double bed, screened-in porch. Nos. 26, 27, 30, and 31	$18.00
FOR TWO PEOPLE—one double bed. Nos. 33, 34, 35, 36, and 37	$15.00

Each person in addition to the rated capacity of cottage, $5.00 per week extra, $1.00 per day ; except 41, 42, and 43 which are $10.00 per week extra, $2.00 per day.

These cottages are booked from Sunday at 3 p.m. to Sunday at 12:00 noon for a week. An extra charge will be made if cottage is not vacated promptly at 12:00 noon on Sundays. They are furnished with ice box, tables, chairs, dishes, cooking utensils, beds and mattresses. You furnish your bedding, linens, pillows, silverware, etc.

With due respect to the rights of others, all lights must be out and absolute quiet prevail after 1:30 a.m.

A deposit of $5.00 is required to reserve a cottage.

Any cottage not occupied before 9:00 p.m. Sunday will be considered vacated and the deposit forfeited.

Cottage is to be left in as good condition as when rented or the deposit will be held.

No bathing or beach parties allowed after 12:00 midnight.

Cottages available from May 15th to Sept. 15th.

Anyone not registering properly or not keeping a clean, respectable or satisfactory place will be requested to vacate.

Laundry room with hot water and electric washing machine available.

If interested in a reservation mail your deposit, giving the size cottage you wish or the number of the cottage together with the dates required. We can then give you the nearest thing available. The cottages of each group are very much alike.

Water and sinks are being installed in cottages 12 to 37.

Hot water is being installed in cottages 1 to 30.

Changes and improvements are being made on large cottages 3 to 11.

May 1, 1948   LEWIS KOPP & SONS

A printout of the 1948 season rental prices for Chestnut Grove. *Ashtabula Historical Society, Jennie Munger Gregory Museum GOTL Files.*

room variety. They offered shelves for dishes and pots, a two-burner oil stove and, in later years, an icebox. The screened-in porch served as a living room. Communal outhouses were available for all campers near the center of the park. Although the accommodations here were not fancy, especially compared to the elaborate inns in town, families enjoyed themselves as much as, if not more than, any other GOTL guests.

For the most part, families stayed near the Grove and along the water's edge. The beach area was thought to be one of the most beautiful of its time. Baseball fields and a rather large stadium, referred to as "the mansion," were added in later years. The 1951–52 season even included a real dirt track raceway, located where the new flea market is being built coming into town. Families were usually content to just be in the Grove. While dads fished and moms visited, kids ran up and down the little lanes of the camp.

Nightlife included sitting around a campfire or listening to the jukebox in the little general store in the campgrounds. However, as children grew to teenagers, the lure of the strip was always in mind. Edie Chase, a former Grover, explained that

Small cottages in Chestnut Grove. The cottages were neither large nor fancy. Yet for many they were considered paradise. *Cleveland Press Collection, courtesy of CSU Michael Schwartz Library, Special Collections.*

"[the strip] with bright lights, wonderful smells and forbidden mystery at sundown" was always an attraction to the youngsters of the day.

Friendships were forged here that would last a lifetime. The teenage crowd of Chestnut Grove's heyday found their first summer loves. Family memories were created here that would be forever talked about on cold winter nights at home. For many, the days at Chestnut Grove were the best days of their lives. It is no wonder that the campground was referred to as "the poor man's Disney World." Yet like many other places of the past, Chestnut Grove and its beauty did not last forever, and the heartbreak of the Grovers would be severe.

THE ENDING

In 1964, after much deliberation, the Kopp family sold the land to Geneva Point investors for $525,000. The company from Pittsburgh had eyed the property for some time and wished to acquire it to build an amusement park there. However, two years after Geneva Point investors took ownership, the Ohio Department of Parks and Recreation sought to acquire the land. It offered the company $700,000 for the land and cottages. However, the company would not sell, and the state was forced to use its power of eminent domain. In 1966, the state obtained final ownership for $925,000. The actual park would not be constructed until 1977. The lodge was constructed in 2004.

Above: A dozer rolling toward a cabin in Chestnut Grove. *Cleveland Press Collection, courtesy of CSU Michael Schwartz Library, Special Collections.*

Left: These refrigerators were the only pieces left standing after the dozers were finished. Because the doors were left on, the new owners would be warned of serious safety hazards. *Cleveland Press Collection, courtesy of CSU Michael Schwartz Library, Special Collections.*

Another dozer begins work on the Chestnut Grove Beach. *Cleveland Press Collection, courtesy of CSU Michael Schwartz Library, Special Collections.*

In the meantime, families were sent notification letters on the closing of Chestnut Grove. Joe Parry, who had vacationed at the Grove as a child and continued to bring his own family, remembered getting the news. He had been out of town when his wife received the letter. She put off telling Joe the news because she knew that he would be crushed. Joe recalled feeling the wind being knocked out of him upon learning of the park's closing. Hundreds of families experienced similar feelings as they learned of the news. "Home away from home" would be no more.

PRESENT-DAY GROVE

After the closing of the Grove, many families continued to vacation at GOTL. However, the experience was never quite the same. But their love of the lake and all the memories prevailed, and many come back to this day. In 2008, the first Chestnut Grove reunion was held. A Facebook page was created for folks to share memories. Many Grovers have retired to the area and have since become active citizens.

CHAPTER 9

AMUSING AMUSEMENTS

By day, families would sun themselves on the long sandy beaches of the lake. Children would splash in the cool water and wave to the sailboats going by. Moms would busy themselves preparing for a lunchtime picnic under the nearby trees. Dads would discuss politics as they stole glances at the pretty ladies on the beach.

Meanwhile, up the hill from the beaches, new development was taking place along what affectionately became known as "the strip." With the flux of guests in town, business owners wished to provide entertainment for every type of guest. Snack stands, open-air restaurants, rides, slides and midway games began to light up the mile-long stretch of land along Lake Road. For the livelier crowds, bars and clubs opened up as well. So began the tradition of "going uptown" during the evening hours.

The Heyday

Geneva on the Lake experienced its greatest prosperity during the '40s, '50s and early '60s. Vendors lined the street like a carnival, parking places were scarce and businesses thrived along the strip. The area was bathed in the smell of french fries, cotton candy and car exhaust. The hum of carnival rides, followed by shrieks of delight, rowdy cheers from men taking turns on the tough-man and Bingo numbers being called out, was the background noise of a typical evening spent on the strip. While many such attractions

A crowded GOTL beach. The boat lift was one of many that dotted the shores near GOTL. *Author's collection.*

came and went during this time, several attractions remain today and continue to be favorites among the young and young at heart. Many of today's attractions still hold an appeal like that of the 1950s. This section includes some of the most remembered amusements, as well as some of the longest standing.

GAMES

The Midway

One of the most popular game centers of the '50s was a little nook of entertainment located behind the Fascinations building. This section included many of the popular games of the time, including Fuzzy Face, Don't Spill the Milk, basketball, archery and an assortment of arcade games.

Perhaps one of the most intriguing attractions was the shooting gallery. Here folks could fire guns that shot real .22 short bullets. Winchester guns were chained to the station on a nearly three-foot chain to avoid any mishaps. Shooters paid the game operator a small fee and received the bullets in a straw-like container that was loaded into the gun. Next, as the tension built, the game came to life, with gas flames shooting up on each side of the gallery. The sharp-eyed patron, with excruciating concentration, took aim at the mechanical critters turning on a belt in the middle of the concession. The small blast of the gun followed by the *ping* of metal hitting metal could be heard by anybody in the midway at the time. Hit enough targets, or a specially marked one, and the winner could choose from an assortment of prizes. By 1980, due to gun laws, this type of shooting gallery had been replaced by galleries that shot BB gun caps. The midway shooting gallery was eventually closed down and dismantled, evidently being tossed into storage in an abandoned building.

Luckily, the original midway gallery was found by accident behind the walls of a local restaurant. The new owner of the Sandy Chanty, Pat Bowen, was remodeling her newly purchased restaurant when, to her surprise, she found the old shooting gallery. With some research, Pat learned that this particular model had been constructed in 1929 for Coney Island. GOTL midway operators had purchased the attraction from Coney Island and brought it to the strip in 1938.

Pat was eventually able to have some light repair work completed on the dusty gallery, making it one of the last five working galleries of this type in the entire world. Guests of the restaurant today love to view the attraction and learn of its history.

Fascination

The competitive game known as Fascination was invented in 1920. By the mid-1930s, the game was so popular that it began to appear at World's Fairs. However, Fascination really took off once it was constructed on popular shoreline boardwalks, especially at Atlantic City and New Jersey.

Originally part of the midway, the game in GOTL was constructed in the 1930s and remains a popular attraction today. Players compete to be the first one to light a line vertically, horizontally or diagonally, much like in a Bingo game. In the game of Fascination, however, competitors light their lines by rolling a rubber ball down a narrow table. The ball makes its way down the lane to a series of twenty-five holes, in a five-by-five matrix. The hole the ball drops into will determine which light will light up on the sign above the table. The first to light a line is the winner.

The game is interlocked through an electromechanical mechanism. Typically there are about twenty to fifty tables connected together in a parlor. Thus, the announcer who cheers the players on can see who is in the lead and announce accordingly. The games typically last from about a minute to a minute and a half. Winners would be given either a token or a choice of prize. The next round quickly begins, and a money collector comes around collecting fees.

In the United States, there are only a handful of Fascination games still in existence. One reason for the game's decrease in popularity was the advent of the theme park. With the huge parks came more modern and high-tech games, leaving the older midway games behind the times. The second issue is with the mechanics of the game itself. The main operating systems are created by utilizing relays used in old telephone systems, which are nowadays scarce at best. Many times, the only place to retrieve such devices are through other Fascination game tables, which are also scarce. The third problem, which further removed the game from parks, is the fact that it is quite expensive to operate. According to Randy Senna, owner of a Flippers Fascination in New Jersey, operation costs include "hourly wages of attendants, high electric bills, high square footage requirements resulting in high rents and expensive equipment costs and/or maintenance." Thus, only a handful of vintage Fascination games are in working order in the United States, including the one at GOTL.

Bingo Parlors

In the heyday years, numerous Bingo parlors and halls existed on the strip of GOTL. The game became hugely popular in the Depression era after a carnival operator learned of the game while in Germany. In the 1930s, Bingo game rooms and parlors crept up all over the United States and became an ideal amusement during the time. It provided an inexpensive diversion while presenting a much-needed monetary prize.

By the time the 1940s and '50s rolled around, Bingo was well established as a favorite game for both young and old. Thus, as the crowds came to GOTL, so did the construction of several Bingo parlors. One local reported that "you couldn't swing a cat by the tail without hitting a Bingo Parlor back then."

In the 1950s, Bingo was outlawed in many states, as it was considered gambling by lawmakers. However, many resorts continued to offer the game. Most of the parlors advertised merchandise prizes on their front signs in order to avoid gambling accusations. Also, the owners insisted that they gave a huge percentage of profits to the fire department and other organizations, suggesting that the game was played for charity. In

1952, the *Cleveland Plain Dealer* ran an article concerning suspicions of the many Bingo establishments in GOTL. The paper noted that "the game of chance generally stopped in Ohio, runs big in GOTL."

Nowadays, the Bingo craze is no longer just a resort attraction. Although still a favorite game among many, Bingo games in Ohio are usually conducted at festivals, charity drives, churches and other local functions. Some of the old Bingo parlor buildings are still intact at GOTL. Such buildings include the Shore Shop, the Lollipop Shop and a portion of the current chamber of commerce building.

Penny Arcades

The arcade phenomenon at GOTL began in the mid-1900s. Penny arcades, sprinkled throughout the resort, were game rooms where gaming machines could be played at a cost of anywhere from a penny to a dime. The earliest penny arcade games featured digger cranes that would scoop down and "dig" for a prize. The prizes were usually candy, jacks or card games. Later, pinball swept the entire nation and was added to the game rooms. The prize for early pinball games was to beat a certain score in order to earn a free game.

Mini-Golf

Before the Depression era, miniature golf was in its golden years. With the crash of the economy in the 1930s, the game was nearly lost as an attraction. However, after World War II and the baby boom years, the game quickly became a family favorite once again.

As mentioned earlier, Allison's Miniature Golf course was opened in 1924 and holds the title as the oldest continuously operating mini course in the country. With its current (ninetieth) season underway, the course remains a very special place among guests. Not only is this course a link with GOTL history, but it is also a link in many vacationing families' heritages.

Even the current owners, Georgette and Bill Allison, have longstanding ties with the course. Georgette remembered working as a teen at the "Roll-a-Dog" stand at the entrance of the course. As a young adult, she returned to work weekends to help pay her way through graduate school. In 1981, on their twenty-fifth wedding anniversary, the two purchased the vintage course and continued to update and maintain it.

A postcard for the putt-putt course in GOTL and Ashtabula. Both courses were operated by Erwins and were part of a national chain. *Author's collection.*

Other courses constructed in GOTL included Erwin's Putt-Putt built in 1967. Unlike the family-owned and family-operated Allison's course, Erwin's was constructed as part of a national chain originating in North Carolina. These earlier chain franchises are believed to have originally coined the phrase "putt-putt." This course, like Allison's, makes its claim to fame by being one of the last few surviving of the first chain-type courses. Unfortunately, Erwin's Putt-Putt has been cleared for new development.

In 2004, Adventure Zone was opened, touting a state-of-the-art putt-putt course. This was built on the former horseback riding stables. This putt-putt includes bridges, waterfalls and numerous other spectacular pieces.

The most recent addition to the mini-golf family at GOTL is the grandiose course at Indian Creek Camping Resort.

SPORTING ATTRACTIONS

Bike Tracks

During this time, GOTL hosted two bike tracks. In the 1950s, the bicycle was making a comeback as an adult hobby, whereas in the previous decades bike riding was considered more of a child's activity. As it were, the bike tracks on the strip proved to be a popular attraction for young and old.

The Popcorn Ball was located near the modern-day chamber of commerce and tennis courts. *Ashtabula Historical Society, Jennie Munger Gregory Museum GOTL Files.*

One track was located near Eddie's Grill parking lot (not the lakeside). This track had a huge circle that cyclists could pedal around after renting a bike for the hour. For the less skilled rider or children, there was a smaller inner track. Today, the lane that runs behind the parking lot is known as Bike Lane. The other track was located on the present-day flea market grounds.

Water Attractions

Boating on the lake was and is a very popular activity. Not to be left out, GOTL business owners capitalized on this activity very early on.

In the '50s and '60s, cottage and hotel owners sought to offer a boating attraction from their own waterfront property. Tomas Kainaroi of Uncle Tom's offered a ride to guests. Likewise, Virgil Bogue of Eugobodes was known to invite cabin guests for a ride on his speedboat.

Several business owners bought into the trend and advertised boat rentals. One family created a business around such rentals. On the eastern end of town, past Indian Creek, folks could rent a small white boat with an outboard motor for fishing or sightseeing. Signs could be spotted advertising "Boat Rentals" or "Boats for Hire."

One local business owner set up shop on the beachfront and displayed rafts, blow-up boats and tubes at his shop known as Rent a Float. Meanwhile, the Chestnut Grove General Store offered guests a makeshift

Above: Boats available for rent. *Author's collection.*

Below: Gregory's bathing pavilion, the largest of its time. *John D. "Jack" Sargent Geneva on the Lake Collection.*

raft. This unique raft was actually used during World War II on military transport ships. No matter the historical significance, the Chestnut Grove kids made use of the floatation devices by standing on them and playing "king of the hill."

With time, the motorboat rental trend became a thing of the past. With insurance costs required for this type of entertainment, the owners could no longer afford to continue. As for the raft rental shops, most have disappeared. However, many guests will remember renting tubes and other floats from Allen Court up to a few years ago.

Today, in a similar activity, guests can rent jet skis or pay to go on a charter fishing boat at the marina.

Firemen's Round-up

The Firemen's Round-Up Weekend began in the 1930s. Firemen from several local departments would meet at GOTL and compete in various games, such a tug-o-war, water hose games and relays. The weekend would end with a parade featuring fire trucks, clowns and the newest Miss Geneva on the Lake. The Blazettes would organize food and fundraisers for the weekend. Today, the tradition has resumed for a weekend in June.

Go-Karts

Go-karts first made an appearance in the United States in 1956. By the late 1970s, GOTL had its own go-kart track that replaced the bicycle track in the middle of town. Most thirty-something adults remember the karts being a main attraction and the sound drowning out the strip. Adventure Zone stills offers the attraction, and many still ride them as part of the vacation tradition.

EATERIES

Eddie's Grill (1950)

If GOTL has one icon that represents the town and the atmosphere, it would have to be Eddie's Grill. For almost every GOTL vacationer, a few tunes, a root beer and a dog at Eddie's has and always will be part of the tradition. The little '50s-style diner has a reputation for a fun, laidback atmosphere and a never-changing menu. Yet for many, there seems to be something more than the food and the tunes that bring them to the little orange booths again and again.

For young Eddie Sezon, Geneva on the Lake had been a part of his summers since childhood. Eddie will still tell tales of his days "roaming the streets" of the town. Starting at age twelve, Eddie found a part-time job working the penny arcade at the midway. With a love for the town already in place, and a newfound enjoyment of the business side of it all, a seed was planted in Eddie's heart.

In 1949, a seventeen-year-old Eddie was skimming through the pages of *Popular Mechanics* when an advertisement caught his eye. The ad displayed a picture of a Richardson Root Beer stand. The brand was very well known and liked at the time. Without hesitation, Eddie dashed off a letter of inquiry to the Richardson Company in Rochester, New York. In his letter, Eddie asked how to go about opening his own stand.

Within a few weeks, Richardson responded by sending Eddie materials to start the process of opening and running a stand. As a junior in high school, Eddie set out to open his very own business. With the help of his ever-supportive parents, Eddie laid plans for the 1950 summer season grand opening of his own root beer stand.

Complete blueprints of this RICHardson refreshment stand available for construction.

Go in Business

WITH THIS REAL MONEY MAKER

Open your own roadside stand! It's a profitable enterprise requiring little investment. And your investment is protected by the exclusive RICHardson Root Beer franchise. Many veterans and other progressive business men are making hundreds of dollars a week with the RICHardson refreshment stand . . . and they are having fun, too.

SEND FOR FREE BOOKLET

Free booklet shows layout drawings and gives full details on basic stand and plans for later expansion into a larger stand. Write for your copy today.

RICHardson Corporation
Dept. P-6, Rochester 3, N.Y.

An advertisement for opening a Richardson Root Beer stand, as shown in the June 1949 *Popular Mechanics*.

As luck would have it, one day while exploring lots on which to build the stand, Eddie and his parents noticed a man pounding a "For Rent" sign on a little corner lot. So the family, with Eddie's inspiring determination, rented and built a fourteen-square-foot root beer stand with a root beer barrel and ten stools. In 1950, Eddie opened Eddie's Grill, serving Richardson Root Beer, shakes, french fries, foot longs and a few other grilled items.

Eddie remembers that at the time there were at least

eight restaurants in a row on his side of the street. And it crossed his mind that his tiny little stand would be no match for some of the other eateries. Yet Eddie did not let these obstacles determine his dreams.

As a son of two Slovenian immigrant parents, Eddie had been taught the virtue of a hard work ethic. Eddie will tell anyone today that his parents are his "inspiration" when it comes to dedication and working hard. Throughout the years, as his parents continued to be a huge part of the business, Eddie was always very much in awe of their relentlessness to see the grill succeed.

With each passing summer, Eddie continued, with much help from his parents and siblings, to serve his simple menu, complete with his mom's own coney sauce. His late mother eventually became known as "the Lady in the Window" at the order counter. She maintained her post from 1950 to 2002. Near the back of the restaurant, there are several framed pictures and articles about Mary.

Within a few years of the grand opening of his stand, Eddie was seeing return customers on those old barstools. In 1952, the Dairy Queen franchise was added. Eventually, seating became a "good" problem, and Eddie added his El Patio in 1953. In 1959, the original fourteen-foot stand was largely demolished and rebuilt, along with a back parking area. In 1980, an adjacent pizza parlor was added, followed by a nearby arcade in 1983. As if

Eddie's Grill in the 1950s. Notice the Bingo rooms to the right of the photograph. *Author's collection.*

to demonstrate the popularity of the restaurant, Eddie had to add a 250-car parking lot across the road from the grill.

Eddie credits several factors for his success. First, he believes that his consistent menu and the never-changing '50s atmosphere bring patrons back again and again: "No matter when you come, you know what you will get." Most importantly, Eddie believes that the support of his family was and is the key to success. From the beginning, when the business was in the dreaming stage, all the way through today, when the line to get in wraps around the corner, Eddie knows that he could not manage without the help of his family.

In an article that ran in the *Geneva Gazette*, Eddie's daughter stated that "Eddie's Grill is the fulfillment of 'the American Dream' for him. He started from scratch, from nothing, the son of an immigrant. It just goes to show that with hard work and dedication, you can do anything in America."

Madsen Donuts

In 1936, Carl Madsen and his wife opened a small donut shop in Niles, Ohio. In 1938, they moved the little business to GOTL, never knowing that it would become one of the most beloved food stands for thousands of visitors. Although very famous for his donut recipe, Mr. Madsen is most remembered for remarkable leadership. Mark Brunner, who grew up in GOTL, recalled fond memories of his first boss.

Apparently, "Pappy" Madsen had an orderly system for everything. No job duty was any less important than another. From the donut fillers to the box folders, each job was to be performed with the same expertise. Mark, a successful college professor, credited Pappy for teaching him a hard work ethic and the importance of being a team player.

Between secret recipes and hardworking employees, the donut shop has remained a favorite business for nearly eighty-five years. In 1974, Pappy was ready to retire and sold the shop to the Biery family. Harry and Bev Biery were the perfect couple to buy the shop, as they had loved to visit it as kids. They continued in Pappy's tradition and have kept the recipe and variety of donuts the same.

The Bierys' children all worked in the donut shop as well and recalled spending every summer day there. Keith Biery, current owner as of 2012, met his wife while working there in his teens. The couple purchased the business from Keith's parents and have kept the place virtually the same as in 1936.

In 2009, Madsen Donuts was nominated on Fox Cleveland's Hot List for "Best Donut." Visitors today continue their own love affair with the place and line up in front of the store each and every summer.

Capo's Pizza

Capo's Pizza was started as something of a mistake. In 1964, the Capo family loaded into a car from their home in Pennsylvania and ventured out toward Conneaut Lake Park. Somehow or another, the family found themselves driving down a busy strip. Tony, the son and current owner, remembered his dad remarking that "we could sell some pizzas here."

The family had owned and operated a successful pizza shop in Pennsylvania. Using Frank Capo's own recipe since 1959, the pizza was a huge hit in their hometown. But upon discovering GOTL, Frank wasted no time setting up a shop there. In 1965, Capo's opened on the strip, and hungry guests followed the doughy smell right to the little order window.

In 1991, Frank passed away, leaving the business to his son. Tony still uses his father's secret recipe. It is not unheard of for the shop to sell up to eight hundred slices of pizza on a busy weekend night.

Burn's Texas BBQ

Burn's Texas BBQ was located in the current Corner Store in the 1950s and '60s. At one time, this drive-up restaurant was one of the most popular joints to get a sandwich. Visitors can still enjoy the same sandwich at Mary's Kitchen.

MISCELLANEOUS

Play Tog's

For many years, tourists would utilize "the white building with Mickey Mouse on the side" as a common landmark. The building stood vacant for as long as most could recall, and new generations of tourists assumed that it was part of the lost era.

A tourist poses in front of Play Tog's. *Jim Lavender GOTL Collection.*

However, the building's owner sat quietly watching tourists pass by from his home behind the old shop. The late Loril L'Hommedieu and wife had once operated a very established business in the large facility.

Loril grew up in nearby Ashtabula Harbor and, in his teen years, worked aboard the famous Ashtabula car ferry. Later, he met his wife, Pauline, at the roller den where she worked. The young couple sustained their family by opening L'Hommedieu Fisheries near the harbor. Once a thriving industry, the fish market soon slowed down after the Depression years. The couple then sought another means of livelihood.

In 1938, the L'Hommedieus leased a shop on the southern side of the strip known as the 19th Hole Beer Garden. In 1939, the couple moved the business across the road, where it would remain for nearly forty-five years.

Eventually, Loril tired of the beer garden and turned his focus to the merchandising spectrum. In the early years, the shop was much like a general store. Folks could purchase anything from toiletries to common kitchen staples. In the 1940s, when the vacationing trend went from staying a whole month to a week, the general store was no longer in such demand. Thus, the L'Hommedieus revamped their business again and opened one of the first T-shirt shops. From there, a successful souvenir business sprouted known as Play Tog's. The shop remained open until the 1980s, when Pauline's health took a turn for the worst.

Loril took to the task of caring for his wife and left the shop boarded up, with all the merchandise still on racks. Loril could not sell the shop that for so many years had sustained his family.

In 1999, Pauline passed away. Around the same time, Loril's health began deteriorating. Folks from around town would often visit Loril, and he would tell of "the good ol' days on the strip." Eventually, Loril made a decision to sell off his property. However, the event would bring Loril back one more time to the days of old. In 2003, the shop was reopened and the cobwebs dusted away. The merchandise of the day remained just as Loril had left it so many years ago. Visitors were delighted to purchase the now vintage souvenirs from the shop. Ashtrays, jewelry and postcards were greedily snatched off the shelves and purchased at the twenty-year-old prices. A favorite item among shoppers was the Jantzens swimwear and sportswear that Play Tog's was once famous for carrying. Loril was delighted to assist shoppers once again.

In 2006, Loril passed away at the age of ninety-eight. Today, the Mickey Mouse artwork has been painted over, and the former Play Tog's building now houses Old and New Antiques.

Geneva Resort Theater

In the 1940s, GOTL housed a successful movie theater. Now PJ's Arcade, the theater's front marquee is intact and in use. Nowadays, the sign boasts of new arcade games and future pool tournaments. However, after the building was used for a movie theater, the sign was known to advertise some quite enticing events.

In 1948, the movie theater was purchased by partners Klumps and Herby. The partners ran a nearby straw-hat theater in Madison on the Lake, Ohio, known as Rabbit Run. The Rabbit was quite successful and drew a large crowd. Thus, the gentlemen saw potential in opening a similar playhouse in GOTL.

On July 16, 1948, the newly renovated one-thousand-seat Geneva Resort Theater opened the curtain to a much-talked-about play called *Arsenic and Old Lace*. The theme was that of a lunatic murderer on the loose, with hilarious twists throughout. For unknown reasons, the summer of '48 was the only year Klumps and Herby owned and operated the playhouse.

From 1949 to 1967, Johnny Kane owned the property. Johnny, who had much experience in show business, knew just the show that the town, especially the gentlemen vacationers, would surely pay to see. In 1949, the Geneva Burlesque was launched, and to the delight of Johnny, it was a huge success. The blinking bulb marquee now invited guests to attend revue shows. Lovely ladies such as Erma the Body and Busty Russel would proudly strut across the stage at the new Burlesque Theater and Cocktail Lounge.

Local resident Jack Sargent still recalls how in his teens he and a few buddies would creep into the burlesque show. Apparently, a great tradeoff would happen on many weekend nights. Jack, who worked at the nearby Ashtabula drive-in theater, would sneak fellows into the drive-in in exchange for the same fellows getting Jack and his friends into the burlesque. All parties were delighted with the trade.

In the 1960s, another popular event took place between the revue shows. Somewhat of the same nature, but toned down a bit, were the Geneva on the Lakes Beauty Pageants held on Wednesday nights. Ladies vacationing for the week would compete to win the pageant of the week in order to move on to the Miss Geneva on the Lake Pageant held at the end of July each summer. All the weekly winners were asked to come back and compete against one another at the last pageant. The winner would then be crowned Miss Geneva on the Lake and would ride in the annual end of summer parade.

In the late '60s, the burlesque and pageants fizzled out with the slowdown of the town. Local resident Pete Macchia purchased the building in 1967

One of many GOTL beauty pageants. Each lovely lady sought to be crowned Miss Geneva on the Lake. *John D. "Jack" Sargent Geneva on the Lake Collection.*

and used it for storage the following seventeen years. The marquee sat dark and blank waiting for its next show.

Alas, in 1984 another idea for the building sprang up. Woods Inc., a local family-owned business, wanted to return the building to its original roots. The family set to renovating the place in order to prepare for the summer busy season. After $60,000 in renovations, the theater was ready to be used as a playhouse once again.

In the summer of 1984, the famous musical *Godspell* was performed on the stage. However, this operation also only lasted one summer. The property was sold back to Pete Macchia, and he once again used it for storage and a possible business rental space.

Another sixteen years passed as the grand theater sat dark and vacant. One cold winter's day, a young couple happened through town. They noticed a "For Lease" sign in what appeared to be a vintage theater. At once, the couple knew that this building and its ideal location was a must-have. They quickly contacted Pete and made preparations for the summer season.

The new lessees were John Bloom and his girlfriend. Bloom, a very talented magician, and his girlfriend renovated the building once again. In the summer of 2000, the couple opened the now six-hundred-seat facility and performed elaborate magic shows that were quite the hit around town. In the last show of the summer, John caught himself on fire as part of his act. He then extinguished himself, pulled out a bouquet and went down on one knee. To the delight of the audience, John pulled out a ring and asked his girlfriend to marry him. Although the Blooms' magic show was a success, it like many others ran for only one summer. Bloom and his wife have become one of the leading American magic acts and are requested by Fortune 500 companies.

As the doors closed once again, Pete's son, P.J., now a young man, hated for the building to sit vacant again. In 2001, P.J. opened P.J.'s Arcade. The game room, located in the front portion of the old theater, remains open to this day. In the back, used for storage, sit rows upon rows of dust-covered folding seats, waiting for guests to return again.

Necessities of Life

Although the resort's main focus was to entertain guests, other necessary businesses did well in these years. GOTL reportedly had three gas stations. General stores and even a pharmacy popped up on the strip as well. Small

GENEVA-ON-THE-LAKE

BUSINESS

	Joe's Fun House	Eugobode
Dave's Dairy Land	Cleveland Inn	Golden Nuggett
Peck's Motel (formely)	Village Hall	Go-Kart Track
Pfister Cottages	Snyder's Cottages	Skillo
O'Niells Landing	Cress Court	The Cove
Popular Breeze Motel	Style's Cottages	Allen Court Cott.
Lake Lane Cottages	Pera's Cottages	Donut Stand
Ford's Cottages	Vallini's Cottages	Log Cabin Inn
Coyne's Cottages & Store	Miller's Cottages	Allen Court Cott.
Jennie Munger Museum	Pera's Motel	Grocery Store
Wigley's Cottages	Skilo	Clark's Motel & Cott.
Otto Court Cottages	Disco	Kramer's Cott.
Shady Beach Cottages	Chicken Coop	Cottages (was Drier's)
Johnston's Cottages	Junk Shop	Uncle Tom's Cott.
Porter's Cottages	Magie Shop	Breen's Cott.
Rawdon's Cottages	Fascination	DiFabio's Restaurant
Thompson's Cottages	Happy Times	Sand's Beach
Chamber of Commerce	Wise's Fudge	Welker's Trailer Park
Flour Box Inn	Roll-a-Dog	and Cottages
Lewis Cottages	Mini-Golf	Surf Motel
Pennsylvania Cottages	Lemonade Stand	The Pub
Swiss Chalet	Barb's Jewelry & Gift Shop	Marino's Cott.
Shore Shop	Jumbo's Joint "T" Shirts	J. P.'s Tavern
Skilo	Madsen Donuts	Pittsburgh Cottages
Popcorn Stand	Putt Putt Golf	Poolside Motel
Time Square	Mini. Golf Course	Schenely Rooms & Cott.
Kiddy Land	19th hole Gulf Course	Varsetti's Lounge
Fortune Teller	King Arthur's Court Motel	Anchor Inn
Ring Toss	Play Tog Shop	Lake Erie Motel
Carriage House	Mapleton Beach Cottages	Jo Jo's Cottages
Shooting Gallery	Eddie's Arcade	Northwind Cottages
Capo's Pizza	Mary's Kitchen	Parkgate Motel
Lake Tavern	Eddie's Grill	Woodbine Beauty Shop &
McCaughy	Theater	Cottages
Mac's Bar	Sunken Bar	Bernard's Cottages
Township Park	Flory's Grocery Store	Hernando's
The Ranch Cott.	Allison's Cottages	Indian Creek Trailer
		Park and Camping

A list of businesses in 1962. *From* Ohio's First Resort: Geneva on the Lake, *1962 visitor's guide.*

grocery markets were quite successful as folks preferred not to lug groceries from home. In the 1960s, the Northeastern Ohio National Bank opened a branch right on the strip.

CHAPTER 10

THE PARTY CROWD

The resort is patronized by the best class of people,
and is run on strictly business and temperance principles.
—Ashtabula County Atlas 1905

G OTL has always been known for its party-like atmosphere. For many,
the fun includes making a loop around the numerous bars and clubs
that line the strip. Most of the bars and taverns that exist today were more
than likely built during the heyday from the '40s to the '60s.

PROHIBITION

The history of alcohol consumption in the town was propelled by many
national events. In the early years of the twentieth century, most public
drinking was reserved for dimly lit lounge areas. Most lounges were a part
of a restaurant separated from the main dining area. Likewise, gentlemen's
parlors or clubs were quiet places for upper-class gentleman to discuss
business and politics while consuming alcohol. Saloons existed at the time
for the "freer" crowd.

Yet in early America, excessive alcohol consumption was viewed as a
problem. Several times in the late 1800s, the "dries" (folks who were anti-
alcohol) protested the producing, selling and drinking of alcohol. It was not
until 1919, with a huge push from the Ohio Anti-Saloon League, that a

national law was passed in America prohibiting the consumption of any and all alcohol. Thus the country entered into the Prohibition era (1919–33).

Although this new law did slow down consumption, it in no way stopped people from drinking. In fact, many new crimes cropped up during this era, including bootlegging, rum-running and operating speakeasies (secret areas to consume alcohol). Given the location of GOTL, it is not surprising that a few members of the town were known to partake in such prohibition crimes.

With easy access to Lake Erie came easy access to prohibition-free Canada. Hundreds of tales exists in Ohio history concerning rum-running from Lake Erie's northern and southern shores. And once the booze was smuggled back to shore, folks needed a place to consume it. Thus, numerous speakeasies cropped up all along the lakeshores.

The most well known of several speakeasies in GOTL was hosted in the Buckeye Hotel. Apparently, on the third floor, a spacious back room worked quite well for just such a place. Gentlemen would gather to discuss important matters, smoke cigars and, of course, sip some Canadian booze. And on the chance that the place was raided, the hotel had a perfect place for hiding the contraband. The rear water tower, having the reservoir tank aligned with the third floor, had an extra inner wall. The bottles could easily be hidden behind the fake wall.

Throughout World War I, the secret consumption of the forbidden drink quietly continued. Enforcing the Eighteenth Amendment meant that the prohibition of alcohol was very costly. Crime rates, including organized crime, grew to record highs. Many of the big business owners made the assertion that the Volstead Act could possibly be the beginning of too much governmental control in Americans' privacy. Thus, in 1933, the Twenty-first Amendment was passed allowing for the sales and distribution of alcohol once again.

BARS, BARS, BARS

Most of the bars in GOTL today were constructed and took off from the '40s to the '60s. As the town flourished with guests in this era, so too did the construction of entertainment facilities for every type of guest. Adding to the drive for bar construction was the lower drinking age in Ohio versus Pennsylvania. Youngsters flocked to the town in order to find a place to party the night away.

The most popular bars of the '50s and '60s included the Barn, the Swallows, the Sunken Bar, Castaways and the Cove.

Castaways Bar was considered to be one of the bars of the day. Many visitors will remember entering through the large tiki head at the entrance of the building. *Cleveland Press Collection, courtesy of CSU Michael Schwartz Library, Special Collections.*

MUSIC

A crucial element in the town's success story, dating back to the beginnings of the resort, is the element of music. From the grand ballrooms with the big bands to the rock banks of today, GOTL has always included music. There were some very famous acts on the stages during the heyday years. From 1900 to the 1940s, Cab Calloway, the Dorsey Brothers, Duke Ellington, Kay Kiser, Glenn Miller, Ozzie and Harriet Nelson and Lawrence Welk occupied the stage. From the 1940s to the 1960s, it was Chubby Checker, Bill Haley and the Comets, the Flamingos, Jaggerz, Tiny Tim, the Platters and the Temptations. And from the late 1960s to 1970s, James Brown, James Gang, Jimi Hendrix and more made their marks.

CHAPTER 11

ERIEVIEW PARK

Perhaps the most well-known and most-beloved GOTL town attraction, spanning four generations of vacationers, was Erieview Park. Until recently, the amusement park was included in everyone's uptown activities. Unfortunately, with the recent downturn in the economy, the little amusement park closed and sold off the vintage rides. Here is a brief history of how the park began, was sustained and was eventually closed forever.

ERIEVIEW PARK TIMELINE: 1920–2010

- 1920: Eusebio and Martha Pera purchase the New Inn in GOTL. The property behind the inn would become the area used to develop the amusement park.

- 1920–25: The Peras clear land and add Pera's Park near the inn: tennis courts, beach access, mini-golf and picnic areas.

- 1928: The Peras open the Breakers Ballroom. The name was chosen by casting votes.

- 1929: The Breakers is renamed the Pier Ballroom. The ballroom would become the most popular dance hall between Sandusky and New York.

Erieview Park on a typical summer evening in the 1980s. *Ashtabula Historical Society, Jennie Munger Gregory Museum GOTL Files.*

- 1941: Eusebio "Pop" and Martha begin plans for a children's amusement area. They build the Dodgem Building. However, World War II halts progress. The Peras open a game center in the Dodgem Building known as Recreation for the Nation. This attraction includes several skee ball tables, duckpin bowling and other popular games.

- 1945: Progress on Kiddie Land resumes. Pera's Kiddie Land opens. The business is successful, allowing the Peras to purchase a new ride each year.

- 1945: Bumper cars are added.

- 1947: The Flying Scooters are added.

- 1948: Hudson-styled kiddie cars are added.

- 1950: The first "haunted house" is purchased from the Pretzel Amusement Ride Company. The scary attraction replaces the old duckpin bowling alley. The Pretzel Haunted House mysteriously catches fire during the first night of operation. Guests are escorted out. The building sustains damage to the roof, but no one is hurt.

Repairs are made, and the attraction continues to entertain visitors for nearly thirty years.

- 1954: Hodge's hand-cranked car ride (a top seller at 2007 auction) is added.

- 1956: The merry-go-round is added.

- 1959: The Ferris wheel (no. 5 model) is added. This particular Ferris wheel, built by the Eli Bridge Company, was one of many constructed by W.E. Sullivan, who became fascinated with Ferris wheels after riding an original George Ferris wheel in 1893. Although his family and friends were skeptical, Sullivan pursued his dream of building his own wheel. After the first success, the Eli Bridge Company became an official manufacturer of the Ferris wheel. The no. 5 Eli model, purchased by the Peras, was actually built as a thrill ride. Riders noticed that the very fast speed was sure to produce butterfly sensations on the downspin.

- 1960: The Wet Boats are added.

- 1962: Martha passes away at age eighty.

- 1964: The Sky Fighter ride is added.

- 1965: The miniature train (purchased from the old Conneaut Park) is added.

- 1969: The Molina and Sons kiddie roller coaster is added.

- 1973: The last dance at Pier Ballroom is held.

Although the park remained a favorite for young families, the Pera family knew that times were a' changing, causing a decrease in the business end of Pera's Kiddie Land. By the early '70s, Pop and Martha's children were heavily involved in the business. As business slowed, the family decided to make some necessary changes to the little park in order to attract more business. Don Woodward, the Peras' grandson, later discussed this issue in the *Gazette* newspaper: "[The park] kept going because it was an attraction.

But if the park hadn't been at Geneva on the Lake, it would have closed…If we were going to survive, we needed to broaden our base a bit."

The matter was settled. The family would expand the park to include adult rides as well. Thus, from the '70s to the late '80s, numerous adult rides were added to the park, including the Octopus, the Tilt-a-Whirl, the Rock and Spin and the Roll-o-Plane.

The timeline continues.

- 1979: The name of the park is changed to Erieview Park.

- 1979: The original Pretzel Haunted House is replaced by Fright Zone Dark Ride.

THE FRIGHT ZONE

Standing in front of the "spook house" looking up at the porch, children watched as the rounded cars were loaded with brave passengers. After buckling them in, the ride attendant would return to a post and push a button. The rounded car, with a ghost face, would creak to life with a small jilt. The car would slowly roll on its small track. Within seconds, riders were approaching the double wooden doors. At this point, there was no turning back. Souls were thrust into complete darkness, not knowing what lay ahead. The smell of mechanical grease and a hint of dry wood would forever be locked in their olfactory memories.

As the car made its way through the attraction, passengers would be thrilled and chilled with light-up displays of pure horror, including a woman being sawed in half, a flying ghost, a zombie playing piano and worst of all a skeleton head that careened right at the front of the car. Meanwhile, the not-so-brave souls, and parents, would wait outside the building watching a mechanical map displayed from the front porch. The map was marked with the name of the scary scenes, and as the cars approached a scene inside a tiny bulb would light up on the map outside. After what seemed like an eternity to the passengers, they would eventually plunge through two more sets of double doors bringing them back to the safety of daylight.

Children who rode this ride in the first years would return to ride it each summer. It became a tradition that guests never tired of. As these early riders grew to adulthood, they waited with anticipation for the summer when their children could take a ride in the haunted house.

Haunted History

The Fright Zone actually came to GOTL by way of last-minute decision making by Donald "Woody" Woodward.

Apparently, Mr. Woodward had traveled to Pittsburgh, Pennsylvania, to attend the closing sale at West View Park. He hoped to purchase some equipment from the shuttered park. As he glanced around at the few remaining items there, his eyes fell on a haunted house attraction. Upon further investigation, Woody learned that the passenger cars parked in front of the house had been constructed by Allan Herschell. Being a great fan of Herschell, Woody quickly made an offer on the cars only. After purchasing the items, Woody returned to GOTL with plans of using the cars in a ride already at Erieview Park.

However, the more Woody thought about the haunted ride sitting in West View, the more he felt a desire to acquire the entire scene set and portable haunted house building. After all, the old Pretzel ride was getting quite out of date. Within a few weeks of the initial sale, Woody contacted the owners of West View Park and thought that he would test them by throwing out a lowball bid. To Woody's sheer surprise, West View readily accepted the offer. In 1977, the Fright Zone became the property of Erieview Park.

The ride came equipped with ten Allan Herschell cars, 540 feet of track, all the mechanical apparatus, the spooky scenes and the portable house. At West View, the ride was a two-story house, but it had to be scaled down in order to fit into the Ohio park. Likewise, while in West View Park, the house had an enormous, man-sized bat guarding the house from the roof. The bat was a trademark of Bill Tracey's work. However, the bat had toppled over and was destroyed in a windstorm before West View closed down. Over the years, the Fright Zone became a favorite among park attendees. Thousands would dare to participate in the creepiest ride in the whole park and return each summer for more.

With time, however, came the slow aging of the ride. Many of the motorized scenes ran on common household appliance motors and wore down after time. The statues of the figures themselves became covered in grime and years upon years' worth of dirt. Plus, many of the figures were constructed out of paper and could barely hold up in the lakefront climate. As one final blow, vandals had contributed to the overall rapid decline of the ride. Evidently, vandalism had always been a threat, as the scenes were not protected by chicken wire, as are most dark rides. Thankfully, in nearby Vienna, Ohio, a group known as DAFE (Dark House and Fun Ride

Enthusiasts) asked permission to restore the Fright Zone. DAFE members realized that this dark ride was a true relic of the past and that none like it existed in the United States.

With some TLC and quite a bit of elbow grease, the DAFE team began the tedious job of cleaning, repairing, repainting and securing the entire ride. The results were astounding, and the ride reclaimed its once vivid and fantastic appearance. Riders over the next few years were delighted to see the improvements made to their favorite ride.

But just like at West View, the Fright Zone would once again lose its home. As the day of the Erieview auction approached, Woody had one huge qualm about this particular ride. He could not bear to see the ride split up and sold by the piece. To imagine the spooky yet somehow charming scenes scattered about was unthinkable. Woody insisted that the ride be sold as a whole.

Fortunately, Woody's fears were set at ease as an antique group from Toledo purchased the entire ride. Over the next few months, Woody made inquiries of the antique company about its plans for the dark ride. Woody informed the group that if the members ever planned to sell the ride in pieces, he would personally buy the complete ride back in order to preserve it in its entirety. Eventually, the ride was sold to a buyer at Conneaut Lake Park in Pennsylvania who remembered experiencing the ride as boy at West View. The new owner, Greg Sutterlin, wishes to the preserve the ride for future generations.

The timeline continues.

- 1983: Pop passes away at age ninety-nine.

- 1986: The Twin Tower Waterslide opens, with slides manufactured by the now defunct Flumes Slides.

- 1989: Woody's World Arcade is constructed on the old Casino dance hall grounds.

- 1994: The Pier Ballroom and contents are auctioned. The ballroom is then razed.

- 1995: The last year that Pop Pera works at the park.

- 1997: Vandals break into Fright Zone and destroy the "graveyard" attraction. They also steal the skeleton head.

- 2001: DAFE volunteers to restore Erieview's Fright Zone. The members clean, repaint and repair all attractions inside and outside the building.

- 2004: The state lodge opens in GOTL, sustaining business for a time at the little amusement park.

- 2006: After a heart-wrenching decision, Don Woodward, owner, decides to close and auction the park.

- 2007: The Ferris wheel is moved to the western end of the property and turned to face Lake Erie.

- 2011: A huge gust of wind moves the Ferris wheel six inches from its base. Cars have to be removed in order to move the wheel back to operating standards.

WHERE ARE THEY NOW?

As crowds gathered that chilly October afternoon, many came to say goodbye to a part of their childhood. At the same time, others came to make purchases at the huge auction. Obviously, the rides would go up on the bidding stage. However, other park memorabilia, such as T-shirts, vending machines and carnival games, was auctioned as well. As the auctioneers started the bidding, the crowd wandered around as the park was sold off piece by piece.

Fortunately, several of the rides stayed local. The Ferris wheel was moved only a few hundred yards from its original base. It was turned to face the lake and is part of the Old Firehouse Winery. It is still a popular attraction, in particular at sunset.

The carousel was moved to Adventure Zone at the western end of the strip. The beloved scenic miniature train was purchased by a resident in nearby Geneva. He plans to reassemble the train and run it in his backyard. Other rides were eagerly snapped up by various small amusement park owners. The Hodge's hand cars, a favorite among bidders, went to Goofy Golf in Sandusky, Ohio. The Allan Herschell Sky Fighter, one of the first rides purchased for Pera's Park, went to Colorado. Likewise, the same out-of-state buyer hauled off the kiddie Ferris wheel as well. The little Allan

The Norton Auctioneers brochure, distributed weeks before the auction. *Author's collection.*

Herschell Wet Boats were shipped to Georgia, and the Allan Herschell Hudson-styled cars found a home in a small park in Minnesota.

Winning bids varied among the rides and equipment pieces. After auction, a press release was sent out listing the closing bids for several of the lots. The following is an excerpt from the 2007 release:

> *Allan Herschell aluminum horse Merry-go-Round selling for $24,500.00, an older Fun House at $8,800.00, a Skyfighter for $9,900.00, a Hampton Roll-o-Plane for $8,250.00, an Old National Train went for $8,250.00.*
>
> *Other ride prices included an Allan Herschell Pony Cart ride for $6,000.00, Allan Herschell Helicopters for $7,150.00, Bisch Flying Scooters for $7,250.00, an Octopus for $7,700.00, Tilt a Whirl for $6,600.00, Allan Herschell Kiddy Cars fetched $9,350.00, Molina Kiddy Coasters at $9,900.00, and a manually operated Hodges Hand Car soared to $9,350.00.*

Twelve skee ball alleys brought from $450 to $880 each. Also sold were the food equipment, tents, memorabilia, signage, games and local collectibles.

CHAPTER 12

THE MAIN ATTRACTION

For the hundredth time beholding it, I feel the thrill of discovery, and drink in the refreshing prospect as with thirsty Old World eyes. "Who poured all that water out there?" a child's question on first seeing the Lake, best embodies the primitive wonderment and pleasure which the sight still retains for me.
—*From "Along an Inland Beach," essay by Edith M. Thomas, Geneva, Ohio, 1883*

Throughout the history of the resort, the most popular attraction has and always will be Lake Erie. After all, lakeside living is what attracted the original vacationers to the town. Likewise, the proximity to Lake Erie continues to attract visitors today. There is just something about this blue lake that fascinates the beholder. Whether it be a peaceful sunset over the waters or a rip-roaring wave display, the lake has always provided live entertainment for folks who stop by the shore.

SUN GLITTER

Gazing at the lake at sunset, vacationers will definitely notice the golden, glittery trail that stretches from the shore, out across the lake and then to the sun. The shimmering trail is hypnotic in its movement with the water. There is scientific reasoning for this beautiful display across the lake.

According to the "Weather Doctor," Keith Heidron, PhD, the glitter is the "composite of innumerable sun glints." These glints are formed by solar rays reflecting onto the wavy water surface. This occurs with a certain slope of the sun and our viewing position on or near the water. Eventually, the sun sinks into the horizon and takes the glitter trail with it until the next day.

LAKE BREEZE

The temperature outside may be sizzling hot, but thankfully the lake provides a gigantic, naturally occurring fan. It is not unheard of for there to be a ten-degree difference in the air near the lake versus the air farther inland. This wonderful cooling phenomenon is formed due to the fact that the lake does not warm as fast as the land around it. This causes high pressure over the lake and low pressure over the land. Thus, water-cooled winds are pushed toward shore, forming the lake breeze.

SANDBARS

Many swimmers make a game of "who can find the sandbars first." To play, swimmers must be careful, as most likely they will cross a stretch of deep water. After swimming out a bit, suddenly the swimmers feel an extra-soft sandy bottom below their feet. This area is very shallow, sometimes only ankle deep.

Scientifically, the swimmers are standing on sand deposits formed by longshore currents. These currents carry lightweight sediment parallel to the beach. The bars form in the shallow, where the underwater part of the waves begins to interfere with the bottom of the lake. Essentially, according to oceansafety.com, a sandbar is "an underwater sand dune that has been built by waves and currents pushing the sand into mounds."

Long Point, Ontario, is believed to have originated as an underwater sandbar. Eventually, it formed a twenty-mile-long stretch, now a sand spit, of land jutting into the lake in the eastern basin. It is believed that it took nearly four thousand years of wind and wave action to create Long Point as it is today, according to Scott Carpenter. This gigantic sandbar is a popular vacation spot for lake lovers. However, this same vacation spot has caused its share of trouble for sailors attempting to maneuver through the area.

Sometimes the sandbars of Lake Erie are referred to as "gravebars." This is due to the fact that these frequently shifting and well-hidden bars can be detrimental for a ship, especially one that is floundering about.

TIDES AND CURRENTS

Throughout Lake Erie, there is an interconnected circulation system powered by wind, waves, river flow and water density fluctuation. The shape of Lake Erie's lakebed, its shores and the human-made structures along the shore influence the path of circulation.

There has always been some confusion as to whether the lake has a regular, predictable current system. In the '70s, lake researchers conducted a study by releasing floating devices of varying weights into the lake. These items were all marked with a number, and each number recorded where it was launched. After several weeks on the lake, the little devices began to take on a predictable pattern, thus indicating that there is a standard flow to the water. However, the currents in Lake Erie can drastically change with weather conditions, particularly winds.

Rip currents are a realistic threat for swimmers and surfers on Lake Erie. Recently, the National Weather Service has begun to alert the public when hazardous rip currents are determined. These types of strong flowing currents are formed under two conditions. One of the causes is lake barriers, such as sand spits. The water rushes up along the shore, but due to the barrier, it cannot flow back out with full energy. Next, water will begin to carve out a channel-like system along the sand spit. Thus, the channel begins rapidly pulling out a flow of water. A rip current now exists.

The second form of rip current is created due to high waves. These rips are most dangerous to swimmers as they usually occur near the shore between the wave break point and water return line. This type can be felt by swimmers as they make their way into the high waves—a feeling of being pulled out to sea. The strongest near-shore rip currents occur when waves appear to be rolling almost perpendicular to shore.

Similar to current studies, there has always been a debate as to whether a tide system exists on the lake. Most scientists will agree that there is a minuscule tide system that occurs but proclaim that it is hardly noticeable to the human eye. Yet anyone who has observed the lake shoreline on a regular basis can attest to a daily pattern of when the lake washes higher onto the beach, particularly at nightfall. The tide system has yet to be proven by actual research.

ICE AGE AND THE MELTDOWN

For the first time in 14 years, Lake Erie has completely frozen.
                                        –Headline News, *2010*

Lake Erie is well known for its recreational prospects in the summertime. However, many people flock to the lake in the winter for fun on the ice. Ice fishing, snowmobiling and photography are just a few activities during the winter months. However, the Ohio Department of Natural Resources warns to take precautions, as ice is never absolutely safe.

Another fantastic event that happens in the icy waters at Geneva State Park Beach is known as the Polar Bear Plunge. In order to raise charity funds for the Special Olympics, people from all over Ohio pledge money for the brave souls who plunge into the frigid water. The event at Geneva is the oldest plunge in the state; 2010 was the fourteenth year of hosting the charity drive. Nowadays, there are many other plunges conducted throughout the state in order to raise funds for charity.

At Geneva State Park Beach, huge machinery is brought in, and swimming areas are drilled into the ice. Next, the crowd of onlookers finds a comfy spot to observe, either on the beach or on huge chunks of ice. A large group of rescuers and emergency personnel line the arch of the ice pond. With the sound of a horn, the brave plungers run into the lake and plunge right in for a refreshing dip in the lake. This event drew a grand crowd of nearly four hundred in the year 2010.

A Chilling Business

While visiting the Ashtabula Maritime Museum, one may hear many stories about icy situations on the lake. From ice-cutting ships to stories of ships becoming stuck for months in the ice, frozen water can produce quite a stir. But for one Ashtabula Maritime Museum volunteer, Willard Giddings, ice, the lake and ships produce quite a unique memory.

As a young man of eleven, Willard took on his first job of selling newspapers to sailors and dockworkers. On one cold, blustery day, Willard was disappointed in the fact that business was very slow, most likely due to the horrid weather. As Willard kicked at the ice chunks gathered on the shore, he had a great realization. His father's ship had been stuck a good ways offshore awaiting a thaw line to get back to harbor.

For the young entrepreneur, the waylaid ship presented a great business opportunity, for these sailors would surely wish to have a newspaper. Without hesitation, Willard made his way across the frozen lake out to his father's ship. Luckily he made this dangerous journey without much trouble and climbed aboard the vessel. His father, understanding the dangers of a frozen lake, forbade Willard to return by way of walking the ice. Willard was to stay put until the ship returned to the harbor.

Meanwhile, back on shore, Willard's mother noted that her son had not returned from his daily job. As hours passed, Mrs. Giddings became increasingly fretful and asked the townsfolk to help look for young Willard. Being in the days of no radio communication, it was impossible to contact Willard's father. A few days passed with no sign of Willard, and the devastated mother concluded the worst. Her young son was gone forever.

Eventually, the winds on the lake changed, and a narrow channel opened for Mr. Gidding's ship, carrying several sailors, cargo and his son to shore. As they docked the vessel, a grief-stricken Mrs. Giddings raced to her husband's arms to deliver the horrible news about Willard. Before she could reach Mr. Giddings, there before her eyes was Willard emerging from the ship. Oh the joy and relief that was felt by the shocked mother!

However, eighty years later, as Willard tells the story to guests in the museum, he doesn't remember so much the delicate crossing of the ice or even the exciting nights spent aboard that old ship. What Willard vividly recalls is that his mother gave him "a second warm reception"—right on the back of his britches!

Story retold by Glenn Beagle, Ashtabula Maritime Museum volunteer and good friend to the late Willard Giddings.

The Meltdown

Any local of GOTL knows when the lake has begun its annual thaw. This knowledge is obtained not by looking at the lake, but rather by hearing it. Once some of the ice breaks up, the waves are free to pick up where they left off in the fall. According to locals, the waves pick up the ice plates and then slam them into the shore. The noise is "like that of a freight train," and "windows in our beachfront house rattle" with each thrash. Another local once stated that the first year he lived on the lake, he went outside "to try and figure out what was causing that deafening commotion."

Also, as the ice is breaking up and being flung into the shore, it begins to build huge walls of ice along the beach. These walls have been known to grow as high as seven feet.

INFAMOUS STORMS

Lake Erie is rumored by sailors to be one of the worst places to be in a storm. That's because the lake is known for its ability to whip up a real gully-whopper of a storm in no time at all. Lake Erie has the record for the most inland sea shipwrecks (about two thousand) in history. This is mainly due to the ferocious, fast-moving storms and Lake Erie's geological features.

STORM SEICHES

Sometimes referred to as lake surges, a lake seiche is perhaps one of the most mind-boggling occurrences on the water. To produce a seiche, wind will blow in a continuous direction for several hours, sometimes for days. Eventually, the lake, acting as a huge bathtub, will begin to build water on one end of the lake. As one end of the lake surges several feet deeper than usual, the opposite end of the lake will experience a rapid decrease in water level, sometimes uncovering yards of land. It is reported that the water can rise up to eight feet within three minutes if conditions are right.

Although interesting to observe, seiches have been known to be extremely destructive. For instance, in 1844 a storm seiche descended on a small lakefront shantytown near Buffalo, New York. Within hours, the town was flooded completely. Seventy-eight perished in this storm. Likewise, a surge in 1928 was responsible for killing eleven people. Recently, in 2009, a surge occurred that lowered the water levels from Toledo to Port Clinton. Several marinas and boat owners reported that boats were grounded in the shallow water. The real problem occurred when the water returned back to normal. Sticking like glue, the clay and muck on the bottom of lake prohibited the boats from rising with the water. Thus, several vessels filled completely with water, causing considerable damage.

WIND AND WAVES: A DEADLY COMBINATION

Lake Erie carries a reputation for extreme conditions that can change within a moment's notice. For instance, some mornings, a lake watcher may rise to find a lake that is as flat and smooth as glass, allowing for one to see the bottom of the lake as if looking in a freshly polished window. However, with a change in wind direction or a fast-moving storm front, this tranquil scene can be whipped into a picture of ferocious fury.

Due to its shallowness and saucerlike shape, Lake Erie can roar to life in even the smallest gale-force winds. For centuries, sailors have revered the lake as a force not to be reckoned with while sailing. Hundreds of accounts have been recorded by sailors as they watched huge waves ravish their ships.

One such incident occurred in 1916. After hanging on to the rigging of his sunken schooner, the *D.L. Filer*, for twelve hours, Captain John Mattison, sole survivor, discussed his Lake Erie storm experience. The captain explained to a reporter from the *Cleveland Leader*, "Call it hell. That partly tells it. I've read sea stories of suffering and hardship. I never believed half of what they said, though. I do now." A few moments after the captain was rescued from the rigging, the entire ship sank.

The day of the storm that claimed the *D.L. Filer* and seven crew members is known in Lake Erie history as "Black Friday," as it is recorded that four storm systems converged across the lake. This storm was the leftovers of the 1916 hurricane in Alabama. After the hurricane plowed through the southern states, the low-pressure system made its way up to the Great Lakes region and continued to blow across the waters. Although not considered a hurricane at this point, the wind sustained at sixty-five to seventy-five miles per hour for several hours. Several vessels were lost that evening, and fifty-eight sailors perished on the open water.

Today, the National Weather Service sends out frequent messages for boaters concerning wave and wind conditions. Often, boaters are advised to stay off the water during such lake occurrences.

Some of highest waves recorded on Lake Erie range from twenty to twenty-five feet. However, some fishermen report waves towering at forty feet. Regardless of the record, Lake Erie has and will continue to produce some of the most feared waves and storms on the Great Lakes.

Winter Storms and Blizzards

Yet another instance of wind and wave destruction is known to wreak havoc on the lake. This type of storm, however, has an added element of destruction: winter weather. The storm of 1913, known as the "Great Lakes Hurricane," was like no other in the amount of damage it produced, both on the lake and on the shore. Twelve commercial lake boats went down, taking 235 sailors with them. On land, freezing water spray, rain and snow coated telephone and electric wires throughout Cleveland. Other parts of eastern Ohio received a snowfall of eighteen to twenty-five inches, while winds raged at an average of seventy-nine miles per hour. The effects of this storm left Cleveland in a shortage for milk and food. Several large buildings collapsed under the weight of the snow. This "Ultimate Storm of 1913" has been unmatched in northeast Ohio history.

The greatest winter storm, the Blizzard of '77, was a blizzard like no other. Hitting all of Ohio and parts of Canada and New York, the howling wall of snow and wind was relentless on the entire area. Lake Erie handled the storm in its own way. According to lakeshore locals, the lake was frozen completely flat. (Usually, the lake forms mounds of ice.) Therefore, the wind, which held a chill of sixty below zero, was able to blow unobstructed at full force toward land. And once the tons of snow piled onto the lake, it was free to blow onto land, burying cars and houses. The storm raged for nearly two days. It is the only storm in history that was declared a natural and national disaster by both the American and Canadian governments.

Tidal Waves and Mystery Waves

Sailors are not the only ones who have tangled with lake waves. Many people on land have experienced the effect of lake swells head-on. One of the most infamous occurrences happened on the Ohio shoreline in 1942. According to an article that ran in the *Star Beacon Journal* titled "The Night Death Came Ashore," a shift in wind patterns and a storm front are believed to have created two monstrous waves that ran their way to shore.

On a peaceful morning on the shores of Geneva on the Lake, Leonard Gaetano was busy welcoming five passengers aboard his new speedboat. After all, the lake was quite tranquil for a leisure ride. As the boat headed out on the lake in a course for Ashtabula Harbor, a cry from the back of the boat was heard. "Look what's coming!" shouted a male passenger. As Gaetano glanced out toward the horizon line, he was stunned to see a fifteen-foot wall of water coming directly at the boat. Gaetano began to turn the boat around and head for shore. However, the speedboat was no match for the fast-moving wave. The wave, spotted seconds earlier, grasped the boat and threw it two hundred feet onto shore. The passengers said that "it was as though a giant hand lifted the boat out of the lake."

The wave, which at the time was referred to as a tidal wave, created a path of destruction one hundred miles long along the lakeshore. It claimed seven lives that day and left boats, piers and beaches completely annihilated. Today, the waves of 1942 are considered to be rogue waves, or mystery waves, instead of tidal waves. These mystery waves appear out of nowhere on a seemingly calm lake. Many scientists speculate that they are produced by storm action miles away.

Although huge in size and destruction, the 1942 wave was most likely produced by an atmospheric condition instead of underwater tidal action. Thus, scientists do not consider the wave a tidal wave by technical definition. However, for those who looked out across the lake nearly seventy years ago, the wave will forever be remembered as Lake Erie's Tidal Wave.

EARTHQUAKES UNDER THE LAKE

Since 1786, nearly two hundred earthquakes have been recorded in the state of Ohio. Although many of these were minor, some Ohio quakes have been known to cause great damage. One of the larger quakes to ever rumble Ohio occurred ten miles north of Ashtabula (in the lake) in 2001, measuring 4.5 on the Richter Scale. People reported feeling the vibrations in Erie, Pennsylvania; Toronto; and all the way down to Canton, Ohio. Likewise, beginning in 1987, a series of small shakes and rumbles were felt along the lake, most centered in Ashtabula.

Although there are numerous potential causes for this activity, many believe that the quakes are due to a major linear line found in deep Precambrian rocks that extends from Akron to Ashtabula County and most likely on out under the lake.

According to Mike Hanson, Ohio Seismic Network coordinator, "This [Eastern Lake] region is indeed susceptible to small earthquakes and occasional damaging ones. Our concern is if the area could generate a larger event that would cause considerable damage but we have no evidence at this time to indicate if or when this might happen."

THE MOST BEAUTIFUL SIGHT

Around dusk on a warm summer night at GOTL, an interesting event happens. For a few minutes, the whole town holds its breath for an instant. For at this time of day, vacationers can be found on or near the shoreline watching the most beloved GOTL event unfold.

Although bittersweet that another day has passed on one's vacation, people cannot help but stare in wonder at the spectacular view produced by the collision of water and sunlight.

As one fan, Jeffery Smith, so perfectly described on bloggingohio.com:

> *All the things I've come to know and love about Ohio, there's one that will always top the list. You can travel all over the world. You can see everything it has to offer. But for sheer, everyday beauty you'll never find anything to surpass Lake Erie sunsets. You may find a lot of things that are equally beautiful, but I'll bet you don't find anything more beautiful repeated in endless variety almost every day. Lake Erie sunsets—there's nothing like them.*

CHAPTER 13

TRAGEDIES

As a busy resort hub on a fast-changing lake crowded with thousands of visitors, accidents and even deaths are bound to happen. Although the following accounts are concentrated on just a few examples, it is important to note that others tragedies have occurred over the years and are no less important. The following accounts were acquired through newspaper archives and historical research. Each example is written in memorial to those who were hurt while visiting GOTL.

EARLY ACCOUNTS

One of the earliest recorded accounts of misery on the lake occurred in 1806 with the accidental death of Little John of Indian Creek.

The next written account came via a telegram and was picked up by the *New York Times* in 1874. A small scow boat by the name of *Pearl* came ashore at GOTL on a cold November's morning. Upon inspection, it was found that a man believed to be J. Graham and a boy about fourteen years old were completely frozen. The boy's body was tied to the rigging, most likely in attempt to keep him safe. The scow was laden with lumber, as if the crew was on a delivery. The last sighting of the boat before washing ashore was at Fairport Harbor. No one was sure where the scow was headed. The mystery deepened when it was discovered that the boat looked as though something had run into it. The scow's condition was recorded as a "complete wreck."

An account of the tragedy is found within the pages of Laura Warner's diary in 1899. She wrote, "Aug 17. A Mr. Wharram was drowned in bathing, just below Truman's." This would be one of many drownings near GOTL.

Boat Sinks

In June 1929, a small scow set out across the waters in front of GOTL. In the small boat sat two young boys (ages eight and thirteen), one adult male and a very heavy pile of stones. The little vessel was making its way toward the man's lakefront property, where he would use the stones to continue building a pier. The youngsters were along to help the neighbor man, most likely in hopes of making a few cents.

Sadly, the little scow never made it to the shore. A little ways out, the boat began to rapidly sink. The boys soon were struggling to stay above the water, while the man attempted to pull them both to safety. However, the struggling and paddling was to no avail. Both boys drowned that fateful day. The man nearly drowned as well but was able to swim to safety soon after the accident.

Teens Electrocuted in Lake

On a warm summer night in 1947, another terrible tragedy took place on the lakeshore. At about 1:00 a.m., a group of teens went down to the beach to chat and enjoy the moonlit night. As it happened, two of the youngsters couldn't resist the warm, frothy water and decided to wade out a bit. They entered the lake near William Reynolds's speedboat dock, close to the boat lift, about forty to fifty feet from shore. As the other teens laughed and cheered the boys on, the unthinkable happened. The boys suddenly noticed a tingling and numbing sensation spread throughout their bodies. Within seconds, both teens were fighting for their lives as an electrical current zapped from the electric boat lift in the lake.

Meanwhile, Reynolds was returning on his speedboat and heard the commotion from the dock. Quickly, he realized what was happening, rushed to shut off the electric power and then attempted to rescue the teens from the water. Both boys were rushed to the nearest residence and received CPR. However, it was too late, and both boys were pronounced dead by a local doctor. Later, it would be determined that cause of death was electrocution.

BEACH BODY

In 1952, a young boy and his older sister were walking along the beach toward the west end of town. As they happily trudged along, the pair spotted an odd-shaped structure near the waterline. As they got closer, their young minds could not comprehend the sight. After a few seconds of shock, they realized that they were looking at a headless corpse. The frightened children ran as fast as they could back to their home on Lake Road. Imagine the commotion as the children told their mother about the body they had found sprawled out on the beach.

Officials soon arrived at the scene. While inspecting the corpse, they found a wallet in the pants pocket of the man. If the story wasn't strange enough already, officials reported that the identification card was that of Mr. Cormick. However, most people involved in the case heartily believed that the body was that of a missing pilot, Mr. Hennessy. Hennessy had crashed his plane fifteen months earlier, and an active search was still underway when the mysterious body was found in GOTL. To this day, many believe that the body was that of the pilot wearing Mr. Cormick's pants.

PLANE CRASH

In 1958, the small GOTL landing strip, known as Argonne Airport, was a busy little terminal during the summer months. Folks who had access to private planes regularly landed at the airport in order to visit the resort strip and beaches.

One such group of friends had just spent a fun-filled June day on the town. As the couples, along with two small children, boarded their plane, they happily discussed all the excitement from the day. The pilot easily readied the plane for takeoff as the others waited for one last glimpse of the town and lake from the air. Soon the small plane lifted from the strip and began to ascend into the clear blue sky. However, something happened in the next few moments that had devastating consequences. About two hundred yards north of the airport, the plane appeared to quickly lose speed until it appeared to stop altogether. The plane plummeted to the ground. The two young husbands, both in their early thirties, were killed in the crash. The two small children sustained critical injuries but miraculously survived the incident.

DEATH JUMP

A few weeks after the deadly plane crash, another tragedy occurred in connection to a plane. In this case, the president of the Geneva Chapter of the Parachute Club of America set out to enjoy a favorite hobby. Douglas Harper, age thirty-two, had routinely enjoyed a parachute jump into the lake from a small plane. In July 1958, Douglas harnessed himself into all the necessary safety equipment needed for the jump, including water life preservers. The pilot and Douglas flew out over the lake, looking for an ideal jumping location. About two miles offshore from GOTL, and 3,500 feet up, Douglas was ready to take the plunge. He then proceeded to exit the plane and make a near perfect parachute jump. Once he landed into the lake, he immediately bobbed up and waved to the pilot, signaling that all was well. Douglas had landed only three-fourths of a mile from the club boat that was to pick him up. However, once the boat reached the location, there was no sign of Douglas. Eventually, the Coast Guard was called in to assist in the search. Five days later, two young boys in a boat discovered a body in the lake. Douglas Harper had drowned in Lake Erie.

MURDER

On a late afternoon, a local proprietor of GOTL, James Dama, drove out to his favorite farm stand near Saybrook to purchase some tomatoes. He had been running a successful popcorn and spaghetti stand on the strip, and he needed the perfectly ripened tomatoes to make more spaghetti sauce. As James made his purchase and began loading his items in the trunk, another fellow approached the car. Within the next few moments, the man got into the car, and the men continued down the road.

Whatever transpired in the car next is a mystery. The two men apparently had an argument, and a scuffle followed. The man fired a gun at Dama. Before all was said and done, Dama wrestled the gun from the man and shot him. The man fled from the car and was believed to have been wounded. Meanwhile, Dama stumbled out of the car and approached the nearest residence. Before slipping into unconsciousness, Dama revealed the name of his attacker as Vencenzo Piazza. Dama died the next day in Ashtabula's hospital.

The shooter was no stranger to crime. Vencenzo Piazza, age sixty, was on the run from the law for a triple murder in Union City, New Jersey, in 1933 and a double murder in Cleveland, Ohio, in 1939. He had evaded law enforcement for years. No one was sure why he was in GOTL at the time. However, it was later determined that he frequented James Dama's business establishment. Police also reasoned that the GOTL shooting of Dama was an attempted robbery.

Vencenzo continued to hide for the next year. However, in the spring of 1942, he was found hiding on a farm in Unionville, New Jersey. Apparently, a young woman had remembered Vencenzo around an abandoned farm when she was a girl. Ten years later, the criminal returned to his hideout, and the woman recognized him from a decade before. Vencenzo was arrested and pleaded guilty to all charges against him.

Train and Car Collision

In June 1963, yet another horrific accident occurred in connection to GOTL. A group of six young women had spent the day at a friend's lakefront home. On that Saturday afternoon, they enjoyed sunbathing and playing in the cool water of Lake Erie. The original plan was for the girls to stay the night with the friends. However, the following day was Father's Day, and the young women decided to head home for the occasion. The drive back home to Youngstown was only about an hour, and the girls felt secure enough to travel home.

As the car made its way out of GOTL and then to Geneva late Saturday night, the girls laughed and replayed the day's events. As they made their way through town to the first set of rail crossings, all was dark, and the girls simply traveled across. However, at the second set of crossings, the Nickel Plate and Steel Line a few blocks away, something went terribly wrong.

Perhaps from the exhilaration of being on a girls' road trip, or maybe from the distraction of the thrill of a perfect day, the driver did not yield to the flashing rail-crossing lights. Witnesses who were behind the victims' car later reported that they were startled when they saw the car begin to cross the tracks.

As the car began the bumpy path across, an eighty-nine-car freight train traveling sixty miles per hour barreled down on the crossing at the exact same time. The car and its occupants did not stand a chance. The train careened right into the center of the car and dragged it about three-fourths of a mile before being able to come to a complete stop. All six young women were killed that warm summer night.

FIRE

Sportland Arcade, 1952

On a busy Fourth of July week in 1952, a huge crowd gathered near the Casino gardens. A spectacular sight was unfolding. But this performance was not part of the regular festivities. On the evening of July 5, firemen worked to put out a huge blaze that was quickly consuming Pera's Sportland penny arcade. The fire was considered a flash fire, meaning that it started and consumed in a flash of time.

Art Taylor, who ran the photo shop across the strip from the arcade, was standing on his steps when a girl ran from the building yelling, "Fire!" Art then noticed that the building was filling quickly with flames. He ran to the nearby fire station and sounded the fire alarm. However, by the time the fire department reached the flames, the building was completely engulfed.

The fire roared for nearly two hours, burning, melting and destroying anything in its path, including nearby telephone lines. Thus, the call to other fire departments for backup was slowed due to the downed phone systems. Eventually, trucks from Saybrook, Ashtabula and Geneva arrived on the scene.

As luck was definitely not on their side, firefighters realized that water pressure was low. Using up more precious moments, the teams had to place an auxiliary pump on the beach and draw up lake water to use to fight the fire.

As the inferno continued, the firefighters realized that the roof of the adjacent building, the Casino dance hall, was beginning to catch fire. The team was able to stop the second building before it, too, became a fire emergency. They also continued to watch other nearby buildings, as the intensity of the arcade fire had potential to start a block fire.

Thankfully, the few people who were in the arcade at the onset of the fire had made it out safely. As it was, the arcade burned to the ground that holiday weekend. Later, firemen raked through the ashes and were able to retrieve some coins and metal cash draw boxes that were still intact. The fire was determined to have originated from unknown causes. However, this would not be the last time that the Pera family would experience a fire. And the next time, almost thirty years later, would be far more sinister in nature.

Arcade Fire No. 2, 1979

At the age of ninety-four, Pop Pera was at home enjoying an evening of relaxing. He had spent the better part of his day seeing to his numerous businesses, now run by the family. Although things were quiet in GOTL, being November, Pop continued to keep a watchful eye on things. So after a rewarding yet exhausting evening, Pop reclined in his easy chair and chatted on the phone to his daughter, who was out of state.

As the chitchat proceeded, there was an abrupt pause on Pop's end. To his unbelieving eyes, he discovered huge flames shooting out of the family's nearby arcade and funhouse.

"It's on fire!" Pop cried into the phone.

Martha, the daughter, knew right away that he was referring to the arcade. "Hang up and call the fire department," she ordered.

Pop called the department and explained the emergency. As he conducted the call, he could feel the heat from the flames warming his living room. He feared that his residence would catch on fire as well. Luckily, that did not happen.

The most devastating aspect of this fire was not so much the $700,000 loss of the arcade. The Peras had survived such a fire in the past. The horrible part of this particular fire was that it had been intentionally started. And it was not the only one that night.

From the years 1977 to 1980, the county of Ashtabula had been hit with a rash of suspected arson fires. Thirty fires had occurred in the area, and twenty-six of them had been in GOTL before the arcade fire. A series of cottages and small house fires had been under investigation in the town. Authorities were convinced that most of the fires were intentional. On the same night as Pera's fire, two Geneva businesses were set on fire as well. Both Geneva stores were completely destroyed.

In the case of the Pera arcade fire, it was later discovered that a local GOTL volunteer fireman was responsible for starting the blaze. Ironically, he was believed to be one of the best firemen on the force. It was reported that he helped control the fire at Pera's, fighting the flames with a vengeance.

CHAPTER 14

DARK TIMES ON THE LAKE

Like any great amusement, GOTL would fall into the pattern of a rise and fall of success and fame. GOTL would be rocketed from a quaint family resort town to a party town to an almost completely abandoned town. Several factors contributed to the near demise of the resort, running from the mid-1960s to the mid-1970s. Natural as well as man-made events would nearly destroy the magic found on the shores of Lake Erie.

DISASTER AREA

In 1972, GOTL's new mayor, John H. Korver, declared the town "a disaster area." After Tropical Storm Agnes of '72 smashed through the Northeast, GOTL's shoreline was nearly obliterated. Korver petitioned the federal government for financial assistance in the hopes of salvaging some of the beaches, boat ramps and picnic areas. Although the storm damage was devastating in nature, several events in the few years before the storm had already set the stage and scenery for the near collapse of the town. Tropical Storm Agnes was the final blow to the town, the straw that *almost* broke the camel's back.

THE DEAD LAKE

Quiet Depletion

When the first settlers arrived on the lakeshore, they were astounded by the abundance of wildlife found in and near Lake Erie. Hundreds of species of fish, in particular, were noted for their endless population and sheer variety. Waterfowl nested and played along the lake as numerous wetlands bordered the shorelines of Lake Erie. Like the Native Americans before them, the new settlers wasted no time in benefiting from the bounty of the lake.

As time wore on, more settlers arrived to the lake area. With these settlers came fantastic ideas on methods to capitalize on the lake and nearby waterways. Mills and dams were quickly constructed along the rivers and streams that flowed into the lake. Forests were cleared in order to construct houses, furniture and, of course, numerous mills and dams. Although it seemed a great venture on these lush green lands, the new construction was quietly deconstructing what nature had already established as a well-oiled machine.

The damming of the rivers and streams not only stopped water flow but also prevented many species of fish from migrating and spawning upstream. Thus, even before the turn of the nineteenth century, many species of fish from the lake were endangered if not driven completely extinct. However, dams and mills seem mild compared to the next wave of damage the lake was to endure.

Dumping Grounds

By the mid-1900s, Lake Erie was a huge hub of commercial activity. The Industrial Revolution was at full throttle, and the lake provided an almost perfect location at which to achieve prosperity during this time. After all, the lake provided a connection to the entire world via the water, especially after the construction of the Saint Lawrence Seaway. Huge ships could now make their way from the Atlantic Ocean through the entire Great Lakes system. Manufacturing companies strategically built their factories right on the lakeshore in order to easily load and unload goods from their docks.

The problems occurred when the companies also discovered a simple and cost-effective way to rid their factories of waste materials. They simply dumped the untreated wastes and chemicals directly into the lake and rivers flowing toward the lake. The manufacturing companies were not alone in being guilty of lake dumping; heavily populated cities also needed easy outlets for their raw sewage.

By the late 1960s, the Cuyahoga River, a much-used dumping area in Cleveland, had demonstrated the severity of the pollution condition by catching on fire numerous times. The fire of 1969 would gain national media attention and call the country into action before it was too late.

Between the fires, the total destruction of the fish and water life population, health alerts and advisories and continuing algae blooms, Lake Erie was referred to as "the sewage system of the Great Lakes." Even Johnny Carson took note of the lake's condition, making jokes on national television that "Lake Erie is the place fish go to die." In 1970, Lake Erie was, by all accounts, declared to be a "dead lake."

WHERE HAVE ALL THE BEACHES GONE?

Anyone who visited GOTL during the early to mid-1900s will remember the expansive sandy beaches that once decorated the shorelines of the town. "Beautiful, soft, ocean-like beaches could be seen all the way up and down the shore," claimed June Eberly, a GOTL vacationer of sixty-five years. Likewise, town local Jack Sargent reminisced about those lovely beaches. "It is the beaches that almost everyone remembers," he stated during a recent interview. So what happened to those paradise-like beaches? What made the lake ragingly swallow up the shoreline at an alarming speed?

Many rumors exist along the Great Lake shore, as the problem is not limited to only GOTL beaches. Some experts claim that Niagara Falls is draining at a faster rate, sucking down shoreline as it empties. Others blame the construction of the Saint Lawrence Seaway for numerous technical reasons. In GOTL, words are often whispered that Geneva State Park and the boat marina are blocking sand from naturally replenishing itself east of the park's property. Regardless of the validity of these rumors, one simple fact remains: the glorious beaches of the past have permanently disappeared due to erosion.

In the case of the rapid shore erosion of the late 1960s to '70s, unusually high water levels can be blamed. According to the Lake County Soil and Water Conservation District, high water levels occurred due to increased rain and snowfall. Also, the level increased due to the upper lakes freezing over, which prevents evaporation. When the lake water is higher, waves will strike directly at the base of slopes and cliffs instead of spreading out energy all over the beach areas. Thus, the cliffs, usually made of soft shale or glacial till, are unable to withstand the constant bombardment and eventually begin to crumble, taking any natural or man-made structure with them.

THE DEAD TOWN

Throughout the history of GOTL, a fine line has existed between family recreation and alcohol-related activities. Even today, the division lingers in the air on a busy Saturday evening. While families are enjoying a round of putt-putt, an open-air bar comes alive with the sounds of rowdy fellows putting back a few rounds. In the 1960s, however, a great tipping of that balance occurred. The partying crowd weighed heavier, and noisier, than the family sect.

The tipping of the scales would be fueled by civil unrest radiating throughout the country. The Vietnam War; the sex, drugs and rock-and-roll revolution; alcohol consumption laws; and rebelliousness toward any governmental authority would combine to spawn the most explosive and media frenzied event in GOTL's history.

THE RIOT OF 1965

On a hot Fourth of July night, the many popular nightclubs and bars were hopping. Teens and other youngsters crowded the scene as the drinking age of 3.2 percent alcohol beer in GOTL was permitted at age eighteen. This law drew countless young people from nearby Pennsylvania, where the drinking age was twenty-one. The alcohol was not the only attraction that drew the fast crowds. The little resort town had been known for some time for its party-like atmosphere, great bands and hip bars.

On that otherwise normal evening, while families enjoyed a night on the strip, a ruckus arose from the eastern end of town. Believing to have originated from the Cove nightclub, swarms of intoxicated young people and boisterous bikers began to demonstrate their rebellion toward anything and everything. Nearby bar patrons from the Swallows and Sunken Bar joined in on the action. Before long, the eastern end of town was in total chaos. Yelling and screaming, along with air horns and smashing of glass, could be heard all the way to the western end

Above: The crowds became out of control, and police officers sought to keep them in line. *Cleveland Press Collection, courtesy of CSU Michael Schwartz Library, Special Collections.*

Below: The Ashtabula County deputy's car was thrashed during the rioting. *Cleveland Press Collection, courtesy of CSU Michael Schwartz Library, Special Collections.*

Young people line up outside the police station while waiting for their rioting friends to be released. *Cleveland Press Collection, courtesy of CSU Michael Schwartz Library, Special Collections.*

of the village. Fistfights broke out, and objects were thrown at anybody who tried to control the situation. The small police force and mayor attempted to maintain some sort of peace, but it was not to be had.

Eventually, at about 2:00 a.m., the mayor called for the assistance of the National Guard.

The lines between truth, rumors and media sensationalism remain blurry at best to this day. One local account of the event described it as "minor," with only thirty-four people being arrested, one person hospitalized and one police car damaged. The informant also stated that the National Guardsmen arrived at 2:00 a.m. and, seeing no critical emergency, left town at 10:00 a.m. On the other hand, *Time* magazine stated in an article two weeks later that "at Geneva on the Lake, some 8,000 students rioted for three hours, mauling three police cruisers and smashing shop windows." Likewise, the *New York Times* noted that "police armed with night sticks and tear gas battled 5,000 college students." Fueling the media frenzy was the fact that four other resorts, two in Ohio, also experienced similar issues over the same weekend. Sadly, no matter what the facts, the damage was done. Geneva on the Lake took on the reputation as a rough, gang-infested, dangerous town. Families, especially with children, would no longer feel safe to walk the strip. That is, of course, if the families were to even visit at all.

PARTY TIME

With the new balance of powers, the resort town quickly saw a change in style and appearance. Lining the strip in the late 1960s were hundreds of motorcycles. Some of those cycles belonged to the much-feared biker gang known as the Hells Angels. Girls and guys alike sporting biker apparel could be spotted walking the street and sitting on the stools at Eddie's Grill.

Meanwhile, businesses, at loss for revenue, began to cater to the rougher crowd. New bars and clubs began to crop up with such names as Psychedelic Lounge and Electric Zoo, hinting at drug-inspired entertainment. In 1966, an article exaggerated that fifty bars could be found on the strip, furthering the party-place reputation. (Actually, there were seventeen bars in 1968.) At the same time, family restaurants, cottages and beach-related concession stands closed their doors for good.

No longer were the sounds of the big bands of the '20s or love ballads of the '50s carried through the streets. Instead, risqué songs performed by artists such as the Rolling Stones, Led Zeppelin and the Beatles were heard up and down the strip. When Led Zeppelin released in 1970 the song "Stairway to Heaven," which eventually became known as "the official hymn of rock-and-roll," the musical rhythms (semimetal, sensuous and frantic) symbolized and sealed the revolution of rock-and-roll.

OTHER FACTORS

Although the riots of 1965 and Lake Erie's pollution issues are most notorious for the decline of GOTL, less noted events occurred that quietly added to the problems for the resort.

For one, a huge change in transportation methods occurred. With the advent of the interstate systems, people were now able to zip across the country in a day's times. For example, many people from Pittsburgh who had frequented GOTL were now able to quickly access the East Coast. Likewise, airplane travel became a national phenomenon. The first jet airliner, the Boeing 707, had been introduced in 1959, demonstrating speed, capacity and comfort. By 1970, airlines had begun to promote affordable air travel for the common man. Families could explore the world, if they were so inclined.

Another complication to the old-style entertainment scene was the concept of Mega Parks. In Ohio, for example, Cedar Point and King's Island offered the biggest and best deals to be had this side of the Grand Canyon. Families who had once stayed a week or more at GOTL now spent vacation time and funds on weekend mini-vacations at the super parks.

Yet another, more personal, issue to the town occurred, to the disappointment of thousands of vacationers. After the effects of beach erosion, the owners of Chestnut Grove decided to sell their property to Geneva Point investors in 1963. The investors continued to buy property in the vicinity of Chestnut Grove and eventually sold all landholdings to the State of Ohio. The state government had been monitoring the area for some time in the hopes of adding a state park to the northeastern portion of the state. As word spread about the final sale of the property, many Chestnut Grove families felt displaced in the town that had become a second home. Adding to the frustration, the plans and construction of the state park would be tangled in governmental legalities for several years.

Likewise, as business slowed, cottages, inns and motel owners could not afford the upkeep required on their properties. Many small cottages fell into disrepair or were sold to local landlords to be opened to yearly tenants. Don Woodward recalled in an article that "property almost could not be given away" at this time.

Last but not least was a slam to the last thriving businesses. The drinking age was raised from eighteen to twenty-one in 1970. Thus, the bars that had held the few remaining visitors would also see a rapid decline in profits. Not only were the families *not* returning, but now the young party crowds were heading elsewhere, too.

DISASTER DECLARATION

With all facets of the decline factored in, was it any wonder why the new GOTL mayor of 1972 took a look around the town and declared it a disaster? Cottages that once had to turn away guests every summer due to high volumes of applicants now stood vacant. Guests continued to call and cancel reservations after yet another pollution scare at the lake. The strip that had once been congested with traffic and pedestrians now looked like a ghost town. It seemed as though Tropical Storm Agnes was actually very symbolic of the town's dire situation. After 102 years operating as a popular resort area, the town was now holding on by a thread.

However, against the rumors of gangs and drugs, terrible lake pollution, emerging competition and a tarnished reputation, one spark of hope remained for the little resort. The powerful feeling of nostalgia would soon bring visitors back to the lake and would save the resort from total collapse.

CHAPTER 15

REVIVAL AND REBIRTH

Memory is a way of holding on to the things you love,
the things you are, the things you never want to lose.
—from the television show The Wonder Years

TO BE OR NOT TO BE

The amusement industry from the late 1960s to the '70s experienced a surge of change that would transform the family entertainment business forever. New interstates connecting to one another, home television sets now used for family entertainment and mega parks emerging everywhere would hugely contribute to the decline of yesterday's amusement parks. Extremely popular parks in Ohio such as Buckeye Lake Park, Euclid Beach Park, Sandy Beach Park and even the one-hundred-year-old Chippewa Lake Park were not immune to the changes taking place in the way Americans spent their leisure time. After years of catering to millions of guests, these parks were faced with the heartbreaking decisions of whether to "stay open one more year or close the gates forever." Due to the changes in society, most parks had no choice but to end the summer season.

With the trouble that GOTL had endured over this same time frame, plus a decline in the amusement industry in general, the town had some decisions to make. Like other Ohio parks and carnivals, the proprietors and locals of the resort recognized the small margin that existed between sink or swim. But unlike other resorts and amusement areas in Ohio, GOTL was able to stay afloat during this turbulent time.

Lake Erie

Having the nation declare Lake Erie a dead lake was the wakeup call that lake lovers and government needed to grasp the dire situation at hand. A once beautiful turquoise-blue lake, thriving with wildlife and visitors alike, sat murkily awaiting its fate.

In the mid-1970s, Americans finally realized that the Great Lakes, Lake Erie in particular, were worth a fight. In 1975, the Lake Erie Committee was formed to protect wildlife in and along the lake. This committee was made up of representatives from each lake-bordering state and Canada. Also, thanks largely to the negative media attention, public awareness grew throughout the country. In the later part of the 1970s, the first clean water act was passed by the federal government. The Clean Water Act of 1977 regulated the way in which factories rid themselves of pollutants. The act also focused on methods of handling other types of pollution problems in the Great Lakes.

Almost immediately, lake water conditions improved. Many endangered fish species, in particularly walleye, began to populate the lake again, to the delight of many fishermen. According to a study conducted in 1980, water tested for mercury came back negative. Algae bloom flares were on the decrease, and factory dumping was becoming a fading habit of the past.

Scientists were realistic, however, in their reports. Although lake conditions were definitely showing improvement, it would be years before the damage could be completely controlled. After all, it took decades for humans to almost destroy the lake; now it would take decades to fix. Still, today governmental agencies and the interested public seek to continue and maintain a healthy lake.

As for the aforementioned difficulties of erosion, new methods were derived to slow beach erosion. In GOTL, for example, beachfront homeowners invested massive amounts of money to install cement seawalls, break walls and jetties in order to preserve what little beach was left. These walls were to help lessen wave energy on the shore and catch sand and sediment before it washed away. Although the walls are effective in slowing down erosion, the method cannot stop it. Plus, construction of the wall is tremendously expensive, as is the frequent maintenance required on the cement.

Meanwhile, business owners sought to stay afloat. With the changing vacation trends, many businesses recognized that they, too, would need to adjust their methods of entertainment. Included is a general list of new and/or improved upon business endeavors of the time.

Buckeye Fair Dreams

In the spring of 1980, a local concession stand owner stood atop a hill looking at his newly purchased 1,210-acre dream. The land, located behind the new flea market on State Route 534, was covered in heavy vegetation, grassy fields and thick trees. However, in a few months' time, the man planned to turn the area into a one-of-a-kind resort playground.

The first phase of his project was to build a grandstand able to seat ten thousand. After all, he would need plenty of room, as he had already booked famous stars such as Johnny Cash, Loretta Lynn and Donna Fargo. Next, he planned on adding a huge parking lot, a paved midway, an entrance road and an exquisite stage.

The first event was to be held in July. The debut launch would be known as the Buckeye Fair. The revenues gained from the event would fund stage two of the project. The next stage would be the core of the man's dreams. He reported to the *Cleveland Plain Dealer* that his property would eventually include "a 50 million dollar recreational center, 500 room hotel, convention

A poster for the spectacular star lineup for the Buckeye Fair. *Jim Lavender GOTL Collection.*

center, and health club." By 1984, he planned to construct a 30,000-square-foot exhibition building, another six 7,500-square-foot exhibition halls, a museum, an oval track, several fishing ponds, softball fields and tennis and racquetball courts. The center would be a year-round facility, and its one key feature would always be the performances of famous country stars.

As the week of the Buckeye Fair moved closer, the man's investors and business partners remained nervous. After all, they would need 100,000 visitors to make any sort of profit. Also, the construction was moving quite slowly due to the very rainy season. They tried to convince the man to hold off another year, but he was not to be deterred.

Posters, fliers and news ads began to flood northeast Ohio. Superstars, circus acts, outrageous exhibits, rides and food galore were on tap for any and all wanting to have a good time.

However, the rains were relentless that summer. Though Johnny Cash and other singers did perform, the 100,000 fans did not all attend. In fact, only 30,000 attended for the entire week. And of those fans, they were met with rain throughout the program, and their vehicles became stuck in one foot of mud on an unfinished parking lot. Word spread of the disaster, and the Buckeye Fair became the Buckeye Flop.

The man with his dreams was now in a nightmare. Investors were demanding their money, and local citizens were not impressed with the huge failure once again for the town. By the next year, the man was being called to court, and his dream was laid to rest.

However, a glimmer of light can be found within this story. Although the man's dream dissipated, the dream itself signified something worthwhile. The Buckeye Fair project demonstrated that the people of GOTL were still dreaming. After all the failures of the last decade, hope for the town was not lost. The man's dream of bringing back the lights and sounds of happier times on the lake were not so far-fetched. Dreams such as this would propel the town back to success.

Erieview Park

The Peras decided to add new adult rides in the 1980s. The former Kiddie Land park became a park for everyone in the family. In 1984, the water slides were constructed and opened for business that same summer. Likewise, Woody's World Arcade opened on the former property of the Casinos Ballroom.

Geneva State Park

The new state park promised to the town a decade before was officially completed and ready for visitors in 1989. The park contained the largest beach in the resort. Campgrounds, fishing grounds and wildlife areas were designed into the park's layout. Geneva State Park encompassed the former Chestnut Grove area.

Geneva Marina

A 375-boat slip marina was also constructed within the state park in 1989. The marina included a quiet harbor and general store on the premises.

Charter Fishing Expeditions

With the construction of the marina and the newly replenished fishing stock in Lake Erie, the fishing charter businesses continued to grow throughout the '80s and '90s. (It remains a very popular activity for guests today.) Locals as well as charter companies began to dock their boats at the marina and advertise fishing expeditions. For a fee, guests could board the boat, usually stocked with fishing supplies, and be taken out to the best fishing spots on the lake. Any fish caught would belong to the paying guests on the charters.

The Old Firehouse Winery

Don Woodward and partners capitalized on the Lake Erie wine trend in 1987. The partners chose to remodel the former GOTL firehouse. Not only was their product locally made wine, a favorite with visitors, but the vintage appeal of the firehouse also further propelled the business. The winery business became an anchor for GOTL, as well as many other Lake Erie communities.

Lodging

As business began to increase, cottage owners began massive overhauls on many of their rentals in the 1980s. New and/or improved motels were appearing throughout the town. The 1980s also ushered in another trend that was circulating the country. Condominiums were going up in many ocean-side resort areas. Landowners in GOTL were not to be left out. In 1989, Sturgeon Point Condominiums was completed, with every luxury offered to buyers.

Amusements

GOTL is well known for its abundance of arcade and game rooms. The high number of arcades in the town is most likely a result of the days of the midway games and penny arcades that were extremely popular on the strip in the 1950s. However, in the '70s and '80s, American teens fell in love with a little system known as Atari. The newly designed game system created a fierce competition for vintage arcade games. Thus, video arcades quickly bought many of the new games offered in the industry. In order to attract patrons, arcade owners installed redemption games, or games that rewarded players based on their scores. Prizes included free games and, more often, tickets to be traded in for prizes. Therefore, the fortuneteller games and shooting galleries of yesterday were soon replaced by the new higher-tech games and an assortment of redemption games. And so GOTL, like many other parks, caught the Pac-Man fever in order to offer the best entertainment experience.

In the 1990s, with the return of the family, Adventure Zone was constructed on the former riding stables land. The new complex is featured as a modern-day improvement at the resort.

Chamber of Commerce

The chamber of commerce was added to the town in 1944. In the 1990s, the chamber became one of the main players in promoting GOTL. Such items as the Summer Concert Series, beautiful brochures and a knowledgeable staff have served to revive the resort area.

Jennie Munger Gregory Museum

The 1823 frame house was left to the Ashtabula Historical Society in 1961 as a headquarters. In the 1990s, the museum became a hub of interest in the community.

Above: The new chamber of commerce sign welcomes guests to town in the 1960s. *Cleveland Press Collection, courtesy of CSU Michael Schwartz Library, Special Collections.*

Below: The 1962 dedication ceremony of the Jennie Munger Gregory Museum and Ashtabula Historical Society headquarters. *Right to left*: Virgil Bogue, Ralph Wilkersons and T.A Browe. *Cleveland Press Collection, courtesy of CSU Michael Schwartz Library, Special Collections.*

THE MAGIC RETURNS

If one factor could be pointed out as having the best effect at saving the resort, it would be nostalgia, according to local Jack Sargent. In the late '70s, near the time the town almost collapsed, families from the early to mid-1900s, wanted to share something unique with their children. As the baby boomers began to have children and the early vacationers have grandchildren, many wanted to share the GOTL experience and magic that they remembered from days on the lakeshore. Indeed, parents and grandparents began to make reservations. Some would try out new rentals available, but most would return to their childhood cottages.

The local media also spurred on the rebirth of the town. From stories and pictures of the 1996 Olympic Torch procession to Governor Taft and his family visiting in 2000, the news media portrayed positive images of the area.

In 2001, an article titled "Memories Relived, Created…at Geneva on the Lake" ran in the *Star Beacon Journal*. The writer quickly discovered from vacationers that nostalgia and memories were at the heart of almost every fan of the resort. Julie Patfield of Madison, Ohio, told the reporter, "It's just not summer until we've come to Geneva on the Lake." Likewise a local artist, Sally Parks, who specialized in paintings of the town, seemed to sum up the feelings of many: "This is a very personal resort. It's the only place you can sit on the same bench at Eddie's Grill that you shared with your grandmother when you were a kid. It's the only place your children can sit on the same seat of the train that you rode when your parents brought you here."

Families were once again filling up cottages and eating donuts as fast as the Madsens could ice them.

BETTER LEFT UNTOUCHED

With the new changes and improvements occurring throughout, some business owners recognized the importance of consistency. One such owner was Eddie Sezon of Eddie's Grill. Eddie believed that people liked the idea that "no matter when you come, you know what you will get." From the menu featuring root beer to bar stools lining the counter, not much has changed in the last sixty years at the eatery. Generations of guests have come to recognize Eddie's Grill as a trademark of GOTL vacationing.

Likewise, many other local establishments have adopted this philosophy of business. Snack shops such as Madsen Donuts and amusements such as Fascination remain nearly unchanged from the former glory days of the resort. As families make their way down the street, many will feel as though they have stepped back in time—a concept the town has capitalized on in the last several years.

CHAPTER 16

PRESENT DAY

B y the year 2000, the resort industry at GOTL had finally reached a stabilized condition. Families were returning year after year. Often a friendly, yet serious, competition surfaced on the orange benches among longtime visitors over who had "stayed at GOTL" the most years. This game, however silly, would demonstrate the pride that people now freely expressed in their favorite vacation spot. As the resort returned to its roots as a quaint vacation destination, new and returning guests continued to fuel the town's economy, furthering development and improvement.

LOVELY LODGING

The roots of GOTL began in its ability to accommodate travelers arriving on the lakeshore. Guests in days of old were most interested in staying in a place that offered the promise of rest, relaxation and enjoyment. And 140 years later, visitors still desire these same characteristics when it comes to lodging.

As the entertainment industry began to flourish once again, property owners began to concentrate on attracting guests. This, in turn, would usher in a new trend in lodging styles for many. Several new condominiums were constructed on both ends of the strip, giving the area a touch of modernism. The Geneva State Lodge not only brought more tourists to the area, but business conferences and workshops are held here on a continual basis as well.

INDIAN CREEK CAMPING

In 1964, Ed Andrus set to the task of creating Ohio's largest campground. The acreage that ambled along Indian Creek had only held an old horse barn. Ed had a vision for his land and began to lay areas for campers. In the first few years, only a handful of tents were pitched along the creek. However, as Ed toured the country's campgrounds, he was inspired to do more. Thus he added new amenities as he could afford them. The once abandoned land has now become a multimillion-dollar industry and one of Ohio's most popular campgrounds.

BED-AND-BREAKFASTS

Just as boardinghouses at the turn of century offered cooked meals, many inns now offer meals, breakfast in particular. Known nowadays as bed-and-breakfasts (B&Bs), these inns offer modern facilities with an old-fashioned touch. Guests are able to check into rooms of varying sizes and utilize

The Park's Lodge changed ownership and name a few times. It went from Collinger's Lodge to Park's Lodge to Ottocourt to the Lake House Inn. Today the Lake House Inn has a small winery and gourmet restaurant on the grounds. It also serves as a B&B and has a cottage area as well. Weddings frequently take place here, as the inn is known for its class and beauty. *John D. "Jack" Sargent Geneva on the Lake Collection.*

"common areas." These designated commons typically include huge dining areas, parlors, dens, libraries, decks and beaches. B&B owners seek to offer hospitality and comfort. According to the founder of europeanrelax.com, Gianluca Talamini, "Today's B&Bs offer a warm and cozy alternative to the corporate hotels or motels. Most pride themselves on being privately owned and operated, as well as offering accommodations in quaint and cozy homes, in locations that offer historical, leisure or small-town attractions."

Eagle Cliff Inn (Beach Club): Dream Big

In 1990, after a few evenings of being coaxed by her husband to go see a "great property in GOTL," Luann Busch halfheartedly agreed to go look at it. After all, Jerry was in the real estate business, and he had a tendency to fall in love with properties that needed some major TLC. But the place in GOTL was like no other. Luann was about to learn just how big of an imagination her husband possessed.

The property Jerry had set his eyes on was originally the Eagle Cliff Hotel. Dating back to the 1890s, the three-story frame structure is one of the oldest in the area. If the Busches were to purchase the real estate, they would get not only the original hotel but also two one-story single-bedroom cottages and three two-story cottages. Also included in this once-in-a-lifetime deal was the ranch home that sits adjacent to the property.

At first sight of the property, Luann didn't know whether to laugh or cry. The hotel itself had not been used since the early '80s. The floor in the front room was completely rotted through. The twelve rooms and two restrooms on the upper two levels left much to be desired. Wallpaper crumbled, and fixtures were rusted completely away. Even Jerry, with his big dreams, was taken aback by the interior. Luckily, however, Jerry followed his heart and, with Luann's nervous blessing, purchased the deteriorating property.

Over the next few years, Jerry, Luann and their daughter would face the ups and downs of owning a business that was thought to be in total disrepair. Often the couple debated selling it. However, the family pushed forward and began to renovate the back cottages. When the economy provided them with low interest rates, the owners refinanced. This provided the extra funding to tackle the monumental task of the hotel renovations.

In 1995, the owners sought to have the property listed on the National Register of Historic Places. This was granted under classification A, which states that the property demonstrates historical value in the fact that it

Eagle Cliff Cottage still stands today. It is the only structure in GOTL listed as a national historical landmark. It is one of the last surviving inns of the town. *Author's collection.*

illustrates the lifestyle and culture of historical GOTL. The inn is believed to be one of the oldest remaining hotels in the resort.

Visiting the Eagle Cliff (aka the Beach Club) today, guests will get a taste of the old-style accommodations with a touch of modern-day class. The twelve bedrooms have now been changed to six stylish modern bedrooms, all with an attached bathroom. The front room, which once had a floor rotted through, is now the main common area. Guests are treated to a hearty yet healthy breakfast to start the day right.

As for Jerry, his dream has been realized. He is often found skillfully singing and strumming his guitar on the front porch. Luann, who had numerous qualms about the place, is known by all for her gift of hospitality. She, too, is often found on the porch, laughing and sharing memories with the guests.

BEACH HOUSE

Another trend in recent years is the desire for folks to purchase and restore deteriorating cottages and boardinghouses. Once the construction is completed, the owners proudly inhabit or rent their beautiful new homes. Visitors will be pleasantly surprised to find modern-day appliances, furniture and, usually, beached-themed décor. Indeed, visitors will feel as if they are staying in a beach house that rivals ocean resorts. Evidence of the trend can be found on the continually expanding website Vacation Rentals By Owners (vrbo.com).

One area in particular that demonstrates this renovation trend is Mapleton Beach. Interestingly, this area, formerly Spencer's Sturgeon Point, was the origin of the resort 140 years ago. Perhaps the beach-style homes here will spur on more renovations in a similar style. Perhaps this is a glimpse of GOTL's future, if history does follow suit.

New Wave of Entertainment

As the resort continues to thrive, new elements of entertainment are added. The Old Firehouse Winery hosts an annual wine festival, drawing new crowds to town each year. The Oak Room has dinner theaters and other special events. Likewise, the Geneva State Lodge and Conference Center accommodates groups, including Polar Bear plungers, and hosts many activities throughout the year. The chamber of commerce oversees a successful flea market every Saturday during the summer. Also, the chamber hosts a summer concert series at the township park that has become a favorite activity among locals and tourists alike.

The glue of the town, Lake Erie, continues to stay alive with boaters, jet skiers and beachgoers. Lake Erie's sport fishing is famous all across the state, and thousands come to fish the Great Lake each year. The marina is a rainbow of colorful boats as people live out their dreams of owning a watercraft. In 2009, the state park boasted a stunning new bike and walking path that runs along the lake from the lodge to the state park beach.

A huge change in the amusement sector was the closing of Erieview Park in 2006. Guests returning to the lake the summer of 2007 were devastated to find that the beloved park had been dismantled and hauled away, leaving a vacant lot. However, with the closing of the park came a promise of new development on the acres of lakefront property. Don Woodward, the landowner, wishes to establish a vacation center known as the Landing. His plan is to include a huge outdoor amphitheater, new shops and restaurants along a shore-like boardwalk, as well as various forms of entertainment.

One of the most notable changes in the town is the push toward year-round activities. In the last few years, several businesses have remained open through the fall months. The Thunder on the Strip and Covered Bridge Festivals are both held in October. The Polar Bear Plunge, the Ice Wine Festival and several other activities at Geneva State Lodge highlight the winter months. With spring comes the awakening of many lodging establishments. Mother's Day weekend has been deemed the official opening day of the resort. This weekend was established in conjunction with the opening of Eddie's Grill.

MOTORCYCLES, HOT RODS AND CLASSICS

The automobile sparked the growth of the resort back in the day. Today, classic car and bike enthusiasts enjoy watching the continual parade of classic vehicles that drive into town. The strip has become a mile-long stage for classic car and bike owners to show off their treasures. In the last few years, the Thunder on the Strip Festival has drawn thousands of bikers to the strip, making it one of the biggest events of the year.

Today, a balance of family entertainment and adult nightlife exists within the town. Each sector seems to have accepted the other as part of the experience. Perhaps they realize that this balance needs to remain in order for the resort to thrive.

BACK TO THE FUTURE

G eneva on the Lake has a history rich in prosperity, hardship and
perseverance. From a little clearing on a bluff designated as picnic
grounds to a strip lined with any and every amusement possible, the town

Three children look out over the lake. *Ashtabula Historical Society, Jennie Munger Gregory Museum GOTL Files.*

Three ladies look for shells on the beach. *Ashtabula Historical Society, Jennie Munger Gregory Museum GOTL Files.*

experienced an extremely fast growth period in its first years as a resort. However, the town would eventually reach a dark place where it seemed that all hope was lost. But the little town, with a nostalgic soul, held tight to its roots and surprised everyone with an ability to stay afloat during hard times. As time marched on, families returned again and again, eventually bringing their children, grandchildren and even great-grandchildren to experience a traditional GOTL vacation. With each new generation, new memories are created to be told and retold at family gatherings. Whether it is an exciting day at the beach or a night on the town, one factor remains the same: Geneva on the Lake will forever capture the hearts of grownups and children alike.

BIBLIOGRAPHY

Ashtabula Historical Society. "Jennie Munger Gregory Museum." March–April 2011. http://ashtcohs.com.

Ashtabula (OH) Star Beacon Journal.

Bed and Breakfast in Europe. http://www.europeandrelax.com.

Camp, Mark J. *Roadside Geology of Ohio.* Missoula, MT: Mountain Pub., 2006.

Carpenter, Scott. *Lake Erie Journal: Guide to the Official Lake Erie Circle Tour.* Millfield, OH: Big River Press, 2001.

Census Online. "Ashtabula Co., Ohio Census Records." http://www.census-online.com/links/OH/Ashtabula.

Cleveland Ledger.

Cleveland (OH) Plain Dealer.

Cleveland Press.

Davis, Rick. "Fright on Lake Erie." Darkride and Funhouse Enthusiasts. http://www.dafe.org.

Francis, David W., and Diane DeMali Francis. *Cleveland Amusement Park Memories: A Nostalgic Look Back at Euclid Beach, Puritas Springs Park, Geauga Lake Park, and Other Classic Parks.* Cleveland, OH: Gray & Company, 2004.

Geneva Gazette.

Hamilton, Barbara J. *Where Have All the Schoolhouses Gone?: The History of the Early Schools of Ashtabula County, From the One- and Two-Room Schools of the 1800s through the 1950s.* Jefferson, OH: Schoolhouse Project, 2004.

Hatcher, Harlan Henthorne. *The Western Reserve the Story of New Connecticut in Ohio.* Indianapolis, IN: Bobbs-Merrill, 1949.

Heirdron, Keith C. "Sun Glitter." May–June 2011. http://www.islandnet.com/~see/weather/elements/glitter.htm.

The Henry Ford: The Life of Henry Ford. http://www.hfmgv.org/exhibits/hf.

Jefferson (OH) Sentinel.

King, John. "Early Passenger Trains." The American Railroads. http://www.american-rails.com.

Kingsley, Ronald F. "Chestnut Grove: An Early 19th-Century Lime Burning Industry in the Connecticut Western Reserve." *North American Archaeologist* 14, no. 1 (1993): 71–85.

Lake County Soil and Water Conservation District. *Along the Shore: Living With Lake Erie as Your Neighbor.* Painsville, OH: Lake County Planning Commission, 2011.

Langmyer, Tom. *Lake Erie: History and Views.* St. Louis, MO: Blue Water Group, 2009.

Large, Moina W. *Index to History of Ashtabula County Ohio by Mrs. Moina W. Large: In Two Volumes Published 1924.* Geneva, OH: Ashtabula County Genealogical Society, 2002.

Lupold, Harry Forrest. *Ohio's Western Reserve a Regional Reader.* Kent, OH: Kent State University Press, 1991.

Martin, Carol J. *Dance Marathons: Performing American Culture of the 1920s and 1930s.* Jackson: University of Mississippi Press, 1994.

New York Times. "Ohio Cleans Up." July 5, 1965.

Ohio Department of Natural Resources. "Geneva State Park." http://www.dnr. state.oh.us.

Ohio Historical Society. "Mystery Wave Sweeps Cleveland." http://www. ohiohistory.org.

Schmidlin, Thomas W. "1916 Deadly Lake Erie Gales." Ohio History Central. Ohio Historical Society. http://www.ohiohistorycentral.org.

Senna, Randy. Flipper's Fascination Games of Wildwood New Jersey. http://www. flippers-fascination.com.

Smith, Bruce B. "Lake Breeze." NOAA—National Oceanic and Atmospheric Administration. http://www.noaa.gov.

Smith, Jeffery. "Lake Erie Sunset." Blogging Ohio. http://www.bloggingohio.com.

Solomon Spalding Home Page. "1878 History of Ashtabula County, Ohio: Part 2." http://solomonspalding.com/SRP/saga2/1878Ast2.htm.

Undiscovered Ohio. Cleveland, OH: Thelma Bruce, 1975. Spiral-bound book produced by *Western Reserve* magazine.

United States History. "Prohibition." http://www.u-s-history.com/pages/h1085.html.

"Virgil Bogue." Report in Genealogical Collection Geneva Library, Biographical Vertical File, Geneva, Ohio.

Williams Brothers. *History of Ashtabula County, Ohio: With Illustrations and Biographical Sketches of Its Pioneers and Most Prominent Men.* Philadelphia, PA: Williams Bros., 1878.

ABOUT THE AUTHOR

Wendy Koile lives in southeast Ohio with her husband and daughter, Emma. She holds a master's degree in the teaching of language arts. Currently, she enjoys teaching at Zane State College as a development reading and English teacher. She is also a member of the Not in Our Write Minds writers group of Dover, Ohio. Wendy has vacationed at Geneva on the Lake every year of her life. Wendy continues the tradition with her husband, daughter and extended family.

Visit us at
www.historypress.net